MY LIFE & TIMES

A GUIDED
journal
FOR COLLECTING YOUR
stories

MY LIFE & TIMES

SUNNY MORTON

FAMILY
TREE
BOOKS

Cincinnati, Ohio
shopfamilytree.com

ISBN 13: 978-1-4403-1279-3

15 14 13 12 11   5 4 3 2 1

Distributed in Canada by Fraser Direct
100 Armstrong Ave.
Georgetown, Ontario,
Canada L7G 5S4
Tel: (905) 877-4411

Distributed in the U.K and Europe by F&W Media International, LTD
Brunel House, Forde Close,
Newton Abbot, TQ12 4PU,
United Kingdom
Tel: (+44) 1626 323200,
Fax: (+44) 1626 323319
E-mail: enquiries@fwmedia.com

Distributed in Australia by Capricorn Link
P.O. Box 704, Windsor, NSW
2756 Australia
Tel: (02) 4577-3555

ABOUT THE AUTHOR

Sunny McClellan Morton has been teaching on and writing about the subjects of life story and journaling for more than ten years. She has bachelor's degrees in history and humanities from Brigham Young University and has participated in advanced studies in nineteenth-century women's diaries. Sunny has published nearly fifty magazine articles on genealogy and heritage topics and teaches an eight-week online family history writing workshop for Family Tree University, www.familytreeuniversity.com. She is a member of the Association of Professional Genealogists, National Genealogical Society, and the International Society of Family History Writers and Editors. Sunny shares family stories with her husband, Jeremy, and their three young children. Find weekly tips and inspiration at her personal history blog, www.YourLifein5Minutes.com, and learn more about her at www.sunnymorton.com.

PUBLISHER *Allison Dolan*

EDITED BY *Jacqueline Musser*

DESIGNED BY *Christy Miller*

PRODUCTION COORDINATED BY *Mark Griffin*

contents

1

Gathering Your Family Stories

We share our life stories for many reasons. We want to make sense of the past or relive cherished memories. We want to set the record straight. We want future generations to know us as we really are and benefit from lessons we've learned.

However, writing an entire life story can be intimidating. There is so much to tell—so many details. The project can quickly become overwhelming.

My Life & Times helps you and your loved ones recall and write your life histories in an orderly, step-by-step manner. No need to worry that you won't be able to recall or tell things clearly—you'll get plenty of instruction on reviving your memories and writing them well. Then you'll start filling in genealogical facts, milestone events, and everyday details. With customizable pages, you'll expand on the events that were most important to you, whether it was your high school prom, first job, or that memorable trip to the mountains.

A unique feature of this book is that it also helps you document relationships and values that have shaped your life. Use the flexible format to easily describe your family structure, whether it's a two-parent family with eight children or a blended family with eight grandparents. Pay tribute to those who have influenced your life at critical times: relatives, coaches, teachers, roommates, and friends. Document the values, beliefs, and other principles that have been important to you.

The flexible inserts in the book also allow you to make your history a collaborative project. Send any section to someone else—parents, siblings, children, grandchildren, school friends, or neighbors—and ask for their side of the story. The short fill-in format is easy for anyone to complete.

In the end, you'll have a meaningful summary of your life, its lessons, and those who have helped make it special. You'll gain new perspective on past events and relationships. And you will create a priceless keepsake that preserves your personal and family legacy for generations to come.

Answer the questions in each section as best you can. If information is requested that doesn't apply to your situation (like a marriage date for an unmarried romantic partnership), try to provide an answer of some kind rather than leave the section blank (e.g., "not married" or "moved in together spring 1983"). Where information is unknown, indicate that in pencil. You can erase and replace it with better data if and when you find it. At the top of most pages, you'll find a place to enter the date and the name of the person who filled out the form, if it wasn't you.

Rearrange, remove, insert or otherwise change the arrangement of this book as needed. The format should fit your life—not the other way around. If you didn't go to college, take out those pages. If you married and had children before entering the workforce as an older adult, you might place Stories About a Family of Your Own before Stories From Your Professional Life. For events yet to happen in your life, leave those pages in place, ready for your thoughts when the time comes.

In each section, make liberal use of Special Forms to capture unique and significant aspects of your life. The introduction to each chapter provides suggestions on how you might use the pages in that section. Find out more about these pages below.

Finally, send lots of forms to others to fill out, but continue working on this book on your own. Your successful completion of this project does not depend on anyone else. Simply insert others' memories if and when they return their forms.

Special Forms for Your Special Life

No two families are alike! The Special Forms chapter helps you document unique experiences and relationships. Copies of each are printed at the end of the book; print extras from the enclosed CD. To match the paper weight used in this book, print your extra forms on vellum bristol cover stock, 67 lb. weight. Fill out Special Forms and insert them in the chronological or family section that's most appropriate. Special Forms include:

» **Special People.** Document anyone who made your life more meaningful: a favorite extended family member, godparent, teacher, coach, friend, or neighbor. Send these pages to others and ask them to fill them out for you.

» **Special Places**. Describe the campground your family returned to each summer or the café table that became "yours" during that spring in Paris. Special Places don't have to be exotic: They might be a tree house, back porch, or window seat that was your own little hideaway. Special Places might also be used to describe a favorite uncle's house on the coast of Maine or your great-grandfather's farm in West Virginia where the annual family reunion is held.

» **Special Memories.** Commemorate a religious or cultural rite of passage: a First Communion, baptism, bar mitzvah, sweet-sixteen party, quinceañera, or missionary or Peace Corps service. Document a graduation party, bridal or baby shower, the year your team won the big game, your election to student (or city) council, a promotion, or a loved one's wedding. Or write about those everyday moments that became eternal in your memory: baking with your grandmother, late-night chats with dorm buddies, or the morning coffee ritual with your spouse. Send these pages to loved ones with requests that they share any special memory with you, or a specific one you request.

» **Life-Changing Experiences**. Honor events that profoundly changed the way you look at the world or yourself. You might use these pages to document international travel, volunteer work, missionary service, a brush with serious illness or death, or any other type of momentous experience.

» **Flashbulb Memories.** A "flashbulb memory" is your vivid recollection of a highly public event: the first manned moon landing, the assassination of President Kennedy, the Challenger explosion, or the events of September 11, 2001. Where you were, what you were doing, and how you felt tells something about your life and your relationship to the world around you.

» **Memorabilia.** On these pages, adhere copies of documents, photos, postcards, or other images related to that section. Make reduced-sized copies as needed. Caption memorabilia with a description of what it shows and a note stating where the original is. (Valuable original memorabilia should be preserved elsewhere, in an archival environment.)

» **More.** Add these pages whenever your memories take up more than the allotted space on any form. For example, use them as a second or third page to a Flashbulb Memories or Life-Changing Experiences insert. You can also give these to others to fill out about specific events.

» **In Memoriam.** Use these pages to document and honor the passing of a loved one, whether a stillborn child, dear friend, aged relative, or beloved pet.

Of course, there are other more specific events that may have occurred in your life. Find forms for some of these events only on the CD. Print out the forms that apply to you and insert them in the appropriate sections. Forms you'll find only on the CD are:

» Adoption

» Memories of My Child's
  Adoption

» Me and My Child

» Homeschooling

» Summer Camp

» Me and My Teenager

» Travel Log

» The End of Our
  Relationship

» Solo Parenting

» Unemployment

How to Remember Your Life

You may wonder how you will possibly remember all the answers to the questions in this book. You won't—at least, not right away. You'll recall some things in vivid detail, like your first car or the last holiday you spent with your father before he died. But memories of equally meaningful experiences may be embarrassingly fuzzy, like the birth of your first child (especially if you were the one giving birth).

The good news is that the simple process of remembering one thing causes more memories to surface. As you work through this book, you will be prompted to recall important events and everyday details. As you start recalling them, you'll remember other things as well. For example, while thinking about your wedding day, you might recall that your best man was your college roommate. Thinking of your roommate may bring to mind a long-forgotten road trip to Las Vegas. Then you may mentally segue to the aunt you once visited in Las Vegas—another story altogether that is connected by the slender mental thread of Las Vegas.

What do you do with the avalanche of disordered memories that begin to pile up? Organize them in the book. Simply skip around to different chronological sections and record thoughts as they occur. If your memories don't coincide with the memory prompts, use Special Forms like Special Memories and Life-Changing Experiences. If you remember something new about a section you've already completed, add a More page or an appropriate page from your CD into the correct section.

Of course, there will still be things you don't remember, but want to. When that happens, try some of these tried-and-true tricks to fill in your memory gaps:

1. Look through old photos, yearbooks, date books, letters or papers, clothing, jewelry, collections, and other memorabilia.

2. Listen to songs that were popular or that you loved during that time period. This is especially effective for re-creating emotional memories.

3. Travel back to the setting of an event or time period. Walk through your old neighborhood, visit your alma mater, or stop at the courthouse where you were married. If you can't go to the actual place, try re-creating the ambiance: Visit any lake beach or urban street with sights, sounds, and smells that may trigger your memory. You might even use the Street View function on Google maps <maps.google.com> to take a virtual stroll along your old street.

4. Contact someone who was part of your life and reminisce together. (Maybe they'll even fill out a Special Memories page for you!) Be considerate about whom you contact; don't call those whose memories of the time in question may be unpleasant or unresolved.

5. Read more about that time period or place in a local history or in books, such as the *Our American Century* series by Time-Life Books.

In the end, you still won't remember every detail—who does? Every additional memory you bring to the surface is well worth the effort.

Optional Exercises

This section is not meant to distract you from documenting your life stories. Rather, it offers optional exercises to improve your recall and the effectiveness of your writing. Turn to these suggestions when you run out of memories or story-telling energy. Write them in a private notebook or computer file so you feel free to make mistakes, explore the truth of memories or feelings, or go on that angry rant (which probably shouldn't end up in the final version of your book).

1. When you run out of memories about a particular time period or person: Across the top of the page, write the subject you're trying to recall (for example, "Grandma"), and then begin the page with "I remember..." Start writing everything you can remember and keep writing for a solid five or ten minutes. Write everything that comes to mind, even if it's not a complete thought or it doesn't make much sense. Record images, names, feelings, addresses, descriptions, etc. When you run out of memories, start a new sentence with, "I remember..." You might keep writing "I remember I remember I remember I remember" until you actually have a memory to write.

2. When you are overcome with emotion about a subject: Write an imaginary letter. If your emotion is directed at someone, write it to them (this includes God, fate, or the post office.) If your emotion doesn't have a personal target, consider writing an imaginary letter to a good friend. "I am so mad when I think of..." *Do not send this letter.* Just write it and walk away from it. You may want to destroy it immediately. After you've had time to cool off, return to your writing in the book and see what happens.

3. Write about yourself as if you were an outside observer. Choose the perspective of your roommate, boss, younger sister, or anyone who might have known you well during a particular time. Think through the patterns of your daily life, what you did on the weekends, how you dressed, where you hung out and with whom. Describe yourself as others probably saw you: a grassroots activist, a busy mom, an invalid, a churchgoer, a baseball fan. Then write about how you were or weren't what you appeared to be.

Composite Memories

If you're like most people, you don't recall every birthday or Thanksgiving dinner separately. Rather, you have a "composite memory" of many such occasions during your childhood, with a few stories or details that stand out. Your composite memories give a broad sense of what your life was like, so they are valuable. But they can seem too vague without a specific memory attached. Look at the following example (the composite memory comes first, followed by a specific stand-out memory in italics):

My birthday parties were always noisy with relatives. My cousins sang as I blew out candles, laughed while I opened presents, and screamed around the piñata. *One year, we couldn't get the piñata to break. My father took a baseball bat to it. He spun around so hard he fell on the ground as the piñata finally burst open, and candy showered his head.*

The first two sentences, the composite memory of childhood birthdays, are like an outline drawing. The specific anecdote about the piñata colors in the outline. Use both composite memories and stand-out details to form a more complete and vivid picture of your past.

Filled-In Memories

Sometimes you recall one event that meant a lot to you, but can't recall important details. How can you evoke that special weekend trip with your dad without fudging or guessing at the particulars?

Modern memoirists—the really good ones whose personal stories read like the best novels—aren't bothered by having to reinvent details. They care more about communicating the essence of their experience. But you don't have to take any literary license to combine what you do recall with plausible additions. In the following example, the "plausible additions" are italicized:

We drove through the Missouri countryside, *playing hooky from a history conference. Empty straight highways backdropped our easy conversation.* Dad drove. I sat with my feet propped on the dashboard. *We traded turns with the* cassette deck and preached the merits of music that moved us. *His was probably Eric Clapton and lots of jazz. Mine was likely 90-minute mixes of contemporary folk music bummed from college roommates' CDs. We likely stopped for convenience-store snacks all afternoon and licked our fingers over homemade barbecue at a small-town diner.* We returned to the conference well after the evening banquet. I remember the deep joy of feeling that my dad wanted only to be with me.

Note that real memories and guesses—which are acknowledged as such—fuse to create a complete memory that others can appreciate. We understand exactly the meaning of this memory.

Joyful Memories

Everyone has moments (often much longer periods) of joy, quiet contentment, personal triumph, or deep satisfaction. Times when faith or hard work was rewarded, family or friends came through, or a season of life went smoothly. Make sure this "good news" of life is recorded in each season of your life, either in the regular pages or Special Forms. Your admission of happiness—however brief it may be—allows you to relive it and brings hope and happiness to readers who can share it with you.

Privacy and Painful Memories

You may choose not to include certain events or time periods in your life. You have a right to privacy; recording your life story is not a tell-all confessional! The flexible format of this book means you can share only what you want and omit certain pages or sections. Of course, you may decide at a later date that you want to share those things after all; the book format allows you to add on at your discretion. You may discover, in the process of writing, that your losses or pain taught you lessons or built your character in such a way that you want to share those experiences.

When all is said and done, the most important quality of your memories is not their thoroughness, but their honesty and integrity. Your emotional honesty about complicated feelings and hard-learned lessons—along with all the fun stuff—will make readers love you even more and trust what you have to say.

Stories About Others

Many who write their stories wonder how they will approach negative or unhappy truths that involve their loved ones. Write about your mother's alcoholism? Your father's temper? Will you hurt them? Will you anger your siblings? What if you tell about your own youthful transgressions—will you embarrass your parents or friends?

Everyone will solve this dilemma differently. Some prioritize the tender feelings of loved ones; others feel a moral obligation to truth-telling. (Telling a negative story out of jealousy, spite, vengeful feelings, or even righteous indignation isn't the same as a moral obligation to honesty. Readers can sense intent. If yours is not good, the end result will likely reflect more negatively on you than anyone else.)

You probably don't want your life story to read as either an angry rant or a sappy tale in which no character ever steps out of line. Neither attitude does justice to life's complicated events and relationships. Where you cannot be fair or balanced (and nobody is fair and balanced about everything), just say so: "Even years later, I cannot think of that betrayal without venom in my heart." Your honesty alerts your readers (and yourself) that your feelings are sore and your judgment may not be objective or charitable. Your honesty allows your readers to keep trusting you and to judge for themselves if they must.

In the end, this is your version of your life—not your mother's version, not your sister's version. Don't feel you speak for your entire family. Whatever stories you choose to tell, tell them how you experienced them, what you thought or felt. This is your turn to talk, so make the most of it.

Enlisting Help

Others who have contributed to your life story can help you write it! There are forms for your parents, siblings, spouse/partner, and children to fill out about themselves and their relationships with you at different times of your life. When they add their unique voices and perspectives, your life's record becomes more dimensional.

You can also request any kind of memories from anyone with the versatile Special Forms. So think of your favorite stories from the past and who would tell them well. Maybe your aunt would retell the tale of your teenage mom driving the car into the river. Ask your brother to write about the time you wrestled each other down the stairs and accidentally punched a hole in the stairwell wall. Send these pages to your loved one with a specific request and a copy of the Special Memories form, then insert his or her completed pages into the appropriate section of this book.

You can also ask people to help fill the gaps in your own knowledge. Perhaps you don't remember your father well, or the house you lived in when you were five. Ask an older relative to write about your father, or your older sister to recall details about the house.

You might even request the same memories from multiple people. Everyone will remember things differently, and each perspective has value. You and your siblings will recall your childhoods in unique ways. Each high-school roommate or college buddy will have a different take on the times you shared. (Resist the need to try to set the record straight if stories conflict; sometimes the discrepancies are the most interesting and enlightening parts to read!)

To whom might you send pages to fill out? If they are still living, consider your:

1. grandparents and godparents

2. aunts, uncles, and cousins

3. in-laws

4. friends from childhood, school, and adulthood

5. neighbors (past or present)

6. teachers, coaches, counselors, and other mentors

7. coworkers (past or present)

8. fellow members of an organization to which you belonged.

Some people will respond easily when you ask for help. Others will send something very special only after patient persuasion. Still others may prefer you to interview them, then fill out the form on their behalf. Some of your potential contributors may need to have their memories jogged. Try sending a copy of your own memories of the event in question along with a request for theirs. Or try the tricks listed on page 11: look at old photo albums together or visit your old hangout.

Not sure how to ask someone to participate? Send her an e-mail or message her via a social networking site. State briefly what you're working on, and acknowledge her contribution to your life. Ask her to write her memories from a particular event or time period and send it to you by a specific date to encourage her prompt response.

Here's a sample letter of invitation:

Dear Miriam,

I've been writing some of my life stories lately. I'm working on my college years. I know I've thanked you many times for your friendship, but I'm not sure I ever told you how much I loved and admired you.

I hope to include your voice and memories in my life history. Will you please write down a few memories of our time together on the enclosed form? There's an extra page in case you need more room for your thoughts. I've enclosed an envelope you can return them in.

Thank you for sending this back within the next two weeks or so. If you have any questions, just give me a call or e-mail me at …

When she sends you her responses, you can copy them onto a Special Form and note who the information is from. If she doesn't communicate via computer, you can send a letter with the Special Pages form enclosed. Be sure to include a self-addressed stamped envelope so she can easily mail back the response. Or you could arrange a phone interview or meet in person.

Use the Request for Memories chart on the next page to track your requests to others for their help with this project.

Request for Memories

Use this page to keep track of those you've invited to contribute to your *My Life & Times* book. Noting in which section or chapter you plan to place their comments will help you stay organized and ensure that each section has sufficient contributions.

Name	Page/Topic	Date Sent	Date Received

2

Statistics About Me

The purpose of this section is to create a record of your major life events, including birth and adoption, family structure, religious rites, residences, education, employment (including military service), memberships, marriages, and children. More details about these events will be requested in future chapters; this section just collects basic life statistics in one place.

Don't let unknown answers halt your progress. As you move forward through each section of the book, you may recall or discover more information that you can add to this chapter.

Where to Look for Information

Find information requested in this section in a variety of sources, such as:

» Birth certificate

» Adoption papers

» Baby book

» Birth announcement

» Family bible

» Baptismal record

» Church or
   synagogue record

» Medical records

» Medical bills

» School records and
   correspondence

» School grade reports
   and diplomas

» Letters, including
   envelopes

» Bank statements

» Loan applications

» Mortgage documents

» Lease papers

» Court files

» Job applications

» Pay stubs

TIPS

If you need help finding the documents listed on these pages, look carefully through old paperwork. Try looking in these places:
» Check your own files. Don't forget to check the safe!

» Ask others who might have them, especially your parents or siblings. If your parents have passed away, ask whomever handled the estate or emptied their home.

» Request duplicate copies from the originating institution, if possible and practical. Learn more about locating and requesting these records in books like:

- » Employment performance reviews
- » Résumés
- » Government or employment benefits paperwork
- » Copies of tax returns and tax documents
- » Investment applications and statements
- » Military enlistment and discharge papers

- » Military benefits statements
- » Marriage license application and certificate
- » Divorce papers
- » Social security or pension statements
- » Family trees and family group sheets

Special Pages Suggestions

Memorabilia

On Your CD

Adoption
(for your own
or a loved one's)

- » *The Public Record Research Tips Book: Insider Information for Effective Public Record Research* by Michael Sankey (Facts on Demand Press)

- » *The Genealogist's Companion and Sourcebook* by Emily Anne Croom (Betterway Books)
- » *The Family Tree Sourcebook* by Editors of *Family Tree Magazine* (Family Tree Books)

- » *Courthouse Research for Family Historians* by Christine Rose (CR Publications)
- » *Adoption Records Handbook* by Teresa A. Brown (Crary Publications)

Birth

Natural or birth parents should be listed on this page, if known.
Information about adoptive parents is requested on a separate form,
"Adoption," found on your CD.

Name

First   Middle   Last   Suffix(es)

Date of Birth

Day   Month   Year

Place of Birth

Hospital (or other place) ....

Address ....

....

Delivered by ....

Mother's Name

First   Middle   Maiden   Married

Father's Name

First   Middle   Last

Religion and Rites

Religion

Parents' Religious Affiliation(s) ....

....

Local Congregation(s) Attended ....

....

Rites

(Baptism, circumcision, First Communion, confirmation, bar/bat mitzvah,
quinceañera mass, ordinations, etc.)

Rite ....

....

Date   Place   Officiant

....

Witnesses, Godparents, or Other Special Participants

Rite ....

....

Date   Place   Officiant

....

Witnesses, Godparents, or Other Special Participants

Rite ....

....

Date   Place   Officiant

....

Witnesses, Godparents, or Other Special Participants

Find additional copies of this page on your CD.

My Siblings

Name ....

....
Birth Date   Birthplace

Shared Parents   ☐ Mother   If not, mother's name ....
                   ☐ Father   If not, father's name ....

Name ....

....
Birth Date   Birthplace

Shared Parents   ☐ Mother   If not, mother's name ....
                   ☐ Father   If not, father's name ....

Name ....

....
Birth Date   Birthplace

Shared parents   ☐ Mother   If not, mother's name ....
                   ☐ Father   If not, father's name ....

Name ....

....
Birth Date   Birthplace

Shared Parents   ☐ Mother   If not, mother's name ....
                   ☐ Father   If not, father's name ....

Find additional copies of this page on your CD.

Education/Professional Development

....
School Name   Location   Years Attended

....
School Name   Location   Years Attended

....
School Name   Location   Years Attended

....
School Name   Location   Years Attended

....
School Name   Location   Years Attended

....
School Name   Location   Years Attended

....
Degree   Granting Institution   Date Granted

....
Degree   Granting Institution   Date Granted

....
Degree   Granting Institution   Date Granted

....
Professional License/Certification   Granting Organization   Date

....
Professional License/Certification   Granting Organization   Date

....
Professional License/Certification   Granting Organization   Date

Marriages/Partners

Name of Spouse/Partner (include all former surnames)

....

Date of Ceremony and Place ....

If ended, date and how ....

Name of Spouse/Partner (include all former surnames)

....

Date of Ceremony and Place ....

If ended, date and how ....

Name of Spouse/Partner (include all former surnames)

....

Date of Ceremony and Place ....

If ended, date and how ....

Name of Spouse/Partner (include all former surnames)

....

Date of Ceremony and Place ....

If ended, date and how ....

My Children

Name ....
Birth Date, Birthplace ....
Relationship (natural, adoption, foster-, step-, etc.) ....
Child's other parent(s) ....

Name ....
Birth Date, Birthplace ....
Relationship (natural, adoption, foster-, step-, etc.) ....
Child's other parent(s) ....

Name ....
Birth Date, Birthplace ....
Relationship (natural, adoption, foster-, step-, etc.) ....
Child's other parent(s) ....

Name ....
Birth Date, Birthplace ....
Relationship (natural, adoption, foster-, step-, etc.) ....
Child's other parent(s) ....

Name ....
Birth Date, Birthplace ....
Relationship (natural, adoption, foster-, step-, etc.) ....
Child's other parent(s) ....

Name ....
Birth Date, Birth place ....
Relationship (natural, adoption, foster, step-, etc.) ....
Child's other parent(s) ....

Find additional copies of this page on your CD.

Residences

Fill in all your residences since birth, or earliest known.

Full Address ....

Co-Owner(s)/Occupants ....

Rented/Owned? ....

Dates of Residence ....

Full Address ....

Co-Owner(s)/Occupants ....

Rented/Owned? ....

Dates of Residence ....

Full Address ....

Co-Owner(s)/Occupants ....

Rented/Owned? ....

Dates of Residence ....

Full Address ....

Co-Owner(s)/Occupants ....

Rented/Owned? ....

Dates of Residence ....

Full Address ....

Co-Owner(s)/Occupants ....

Rented/Owned? ....

Dates of Residence ....

Residences

Fill in all your residences since birth, or earliest known.

Full Address ....
Co-Owner(s)/Occupants ....
Rented/Owned? ....
Dates of Residence ....

Full Address ....
Co-Owner(s)/Occupants ....
Rented/Owned? ....
Dates of Residence ....

Full Address ....
Co-Owner(s)/Occupants ....
Rented/Owned? ....
Dates of Residence ....

Full Address ....
Co-Owner(s)/Occupants ....
Rented/Owned? ....
Dates of Residence ....

Full Address ....
Co-Owner(s)/Occupants ....
Rented/Owned? ....
Dates of Residence ....

Find additional copies of this page on your CD.

Employment

Do not include military service.

Job Title ....
Company ....
Address ....
Start/End Dates ....

Job Title ....
Company ....
Address ....
Start/End Dates ....

Job Title ....
Company ....
Address ....
Start/End Dates ....

Job Title ....
Company ....
Address ....
Start/End Dates ....

Job Title ....
Company ....
Address ....
Start/End Dates ....

Find additional copies of this page on your CD.

Memberships

Civic, social, school/alumni, service, historical/
genealogical, religious, or other organizations)

Organization (include chapter)

....

Place and Years ....

Position(s) held ....

Organization (include chapter)

....

Place and Years ....

Position(s) held ....

Organization (include chapter)

....

Place and Years ....

Position(s) held ....

Organization (include chapter)

....

Place and Years ....

Position(s) held ....

Organization (include chapter)

....

Place and Years ....

Position(s) held ....

TIP

Attach a copy of a
membership card
or patch, chapter
newsletter, group
photo, or other
mementoes to a
Memorabilia page.

Find additional copies of this page on your CD.

Military Service

| Branch of Service | Enlistment Date | Discharge Date |

Billet (Job rating/training)	Postings (Locations)	Unit	Dates Served

Find additional copies of this page on your CD.

Military Service

Awards and Rank Advancements

Title	Date	Description

Find additional copies of this page on your CD.

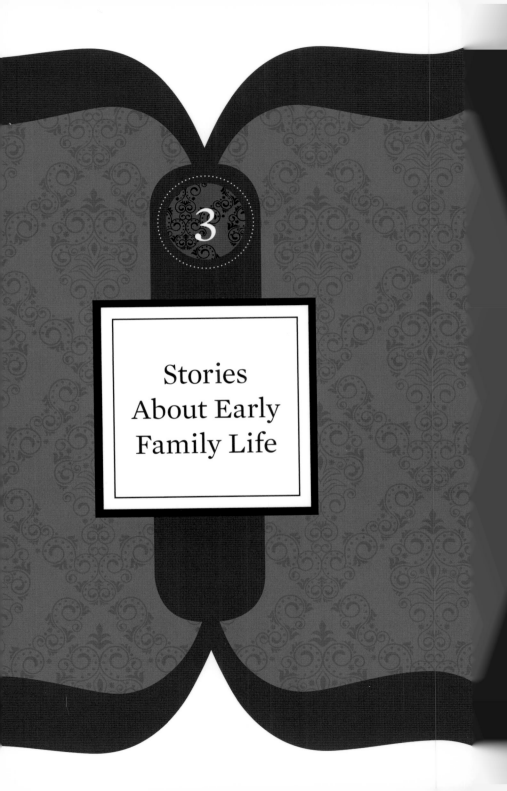

3

Stories About Early Family Life

This chapter helps you write about your parents and siblings and the roles they have played in your life. It helps you gather their memories of themselves and your shared family life, too. Try to document basic statistics (birth, marriage, and death information) for each and every family member, whether or not you are part of each others' lives today. Then add as many details about lives, personality, and relationships as you wish.

When writing about family, you may experience the pleasures of reliving meaningful moments and rich relationships that perhaps you haven't recalled recently. Savor the process of remembering the best times with your loved ones. These memories can enrich your present (and future, through this book) as much as they enriched your past. Describe them with whatever details come to mind: stories, composite memories, or an explanation of how someone made you feel special.

Several of the pages on your parents and siblings are designed to be filled out by them, if possible. You can certainly fill these pages out yourself, but think how valuable it will be to collect your loved ones' descriptions of themselves! The data requested on individual family members (birth, marriage, etc.) may be more accurate if your loved ones fill them out themselves. Certainly capturing their own perspectives—and even their own handwriting—is worth the effort of sending them these pages.

TIPS

» If your parents and/or siblings have passed away and you are lacking information, contact someone who might know: a spouse, child, or another relative. Ask them the information or send a page to them to fill out.

» Use About My Mother and About My Father forms to honor all who have shared those roles in your life, whether natural, adoptive, foster-, or step-parents. Same thing with your siblings (natural, step-, etc). Distinguish between multiple mothers or fathers with an explanatory note at the top of the page (e.g., "this is my father's first wife").

If you need (or prefer) to fill out this information without their assistance, just do your best. If you are grieving the loss of a loved one or the end of a relationship, you may choose to leave that person's description aside for the present. Consider at least writing the basic statistics and (in pencil) a brief statement like, "I can't write about this now without being sad [or angry]." You can say more when you are ready.

If you have a strained relationship with a parent or sibling, see page 14-15 for more advice on writing about difficult subjects. If you really don't want to write your unpleasant feelings, consider giving a short, neutral description based on facts such as, "My sister was tall and good at math."

If this section will stop you in your tracks from recording your life story, then skip it for now and move on to the stories you want to tell.

If you have a strained relationship with a parent or sibling, see page 14-15 for more advice

Special Pages Suggestions

Special People

Special Places

Special Memories

Life-Changing Experiences

Memorabilia

In Memoriam

More

Find extra copies of parent and sibling forms on the CD.

» Remove, duplicate, or adapt sections to fit what you want to say. For example, if your dad was missing from your life, you might remove the page about your relationship. Alternately, you might replace it with a More page that describes the effect of his absence.

» A page doesn't have to be complete in order to include it. Perhaps you know next to nothing about a birth parent, or your parents did not marry or stay together. Consider acknowledging that much on the appropriate form and move on.

About My Mother

Name

....
First   Middle   Maiden   Married

....
Birth Date (Day, Month, Year)

....
Birthplace

....
Death Date   Burial Location

Her Mother

Full Name ....

Race/ethnicity/nationality ....

Birth Date, Birthplace ....

Death Date, Location ....

Her Father

Full Name ....

Race/ethnicity/nationality ....

Birth Date, Birthplace ....

Death Date, Location ....

Raised by (if not parents):

....
Names   Relation

> **TIP**
>
> Memorabilia page with a copy of her birth or infant baptismal certificate or other mementoes relating to information requested on this page. You may fill out additional copies of maternal information forms for step-mothers, birth/adoptive mothers, etc.

Find additional copies of this page on your CD.

About My Mother

Where raised

....
Place(s) (and dates, if more than one place)

....
Place(s) (and dates, if more than one place)

Siblings

Name...

Birth Date, Birthplace ....

Spouse ....

Death Date, Place ....

Name...

Birth Date, Birthplace...

Spouse..

Death Date, Place ....

Name...

Birth Date, Birthplace ....

Spouse ....

Death Date, Place ....

Name...

Birth Date, Birthplace ....

Spouse ....

Death Date, Place ....

Find additional copies of this page on your CD.

About My Mother

Religion

Her family's religious denomination ··

Name of Congregation ···

Education

··

School Name   Place   Years Attended

··

School Name   Place   Years Attended

··

School Name   Place   Years Attended

··

School Name   Place   Years Attended

··

School Name   Place   Years Attended

Residences (not including places lived with my father)

··

Address   Years   Description

··

Address   Years   Description

··

Address   Years   Description

··

Address   Years   Description

··

Address   Years   Description

Find additional copies of this page on your CD.

About My Mother

Additional Marriages (not including marriage to my father)

Name of Spouse/Partner (include all former surnames)

....

Date of Ceremony and Place ....

If ended, date and how..

Name of Spouse/Partner (include all former surnames)

....

Date of Ceremony and Place ....

If ended, date and how..

Name of Spouse/Partner (include all former surnames)

....

Date of Ceremony and Place ....

If ended, date and how..

Name of Spouse/Partner (include all former surnames)

....

Date of Ceremony and Place ....

If ended, date and how..

My Mother's Childhood Stories

Who was she named after?

How does she feel about her name?

....

....

....

....

TIP

Insert a Memorabilia page with photos of your mother at different ages. If your mother is still living, have her complete this form about herself, if possible.

What was she like as a child? Describe her appearance and personality.

....

....

....

....

Describe her childhood home(s) and neighborhood(s). Tell about any place in her home, yard, or neighborhood that was special to her.

....

....

....

Describe her upbringing: how she was raised, her financial circumstances, family health issues, or other significant things that shaped her as a person.

....

....

....

Find additional copies of this page on your CD.

My Mother: During My Childhood

Complete this form if your mother was alive during your childhood. If your mother is still living, have her complete this form about herself, if possible.

What was your mother's daily life like while you were growing up?
(Think about her employment, parenting, volunteering, recreation, travel, etc.)

....

....

Describe her health during these years (well-being, illnesses, injuries).

....

....

What were her greatest challenges during these years?

....

....

What were her triumphs or successes during these years?

....

....

What were her most rewarding relationships during these years?
Her most difficult ones?

....

....

What were your mother's greatest goals or hopes during these years?
Were they realized?

....

....

Find additional copies of this page on your CD.

Me & My Mother: Childhood

Describe the time you spent with your mother during your childhood. What did you do together? Did you enjoy it? Did you spend enough time together?

....

....

....

....

....

....

....

....

....

....

....

....

How did your mother show she cared about you?

....

....

....

....

....

....

TIP

Send the companion form, Me and My Child, to your mother to fill out. Send Special Forms for her to document additional recollections.

Find additional copies of this page on your CD.

Me & My Mother: Childhood

How did your mother discipline you? What did you think about her discipline methods then? What do you think now?

....
....
....
....
....

How did your mother's opinions or beliefs (religious, cultural, social, political, etc.) affect you as a child?

....
....
....
....
....
....

Write any favorite memories of you and your mother during your childhood.

....
....
....
....
....

Find additional copies of this page on your CD.

About My Father

Name

....

First   Middle   Last

....

Birth Date (Day, Month, Year)

....

Birthplace

....

Death Date   Burial Location

His Mother

Full Name ....

Race/ethnicity/nationality ....

Birth Date, Birthplace ....

Death Date, Location ....

His Father

Full Name ....

Race/ethnicity/nationality ....

Birth Date, Birthplace..................................

Death Date, Location ....

Raised by (if not parents):

....

Names   Relation

TIP

Insert a Memorabilia page with a copy of your father's birth or infant baptismal certificate or other mementoes relating to information requested on this page. You may fill out additional copies of paternal information forms for step-fathers, birth/adoptive fathers, etc.

Find additional copies of this page on your CD.

About My Father

Where raised

....

Place(s) (and dates, if more than one place)

....

Place(s) (and dates, if more than one place)

Siblings

Name ....

Birth Date, Birthplace ....

Spouse ....

Death Date, Place ....

Name ....

Birth Date, Birthplace ....

Spouse ....

Death Date, Place ....

Name ....

Birth Date, Birthplace ....

Spouse ....

Death Date, Place ....

Name ....

Birth Date, Birthplace ....

Spouse ....

Death Date, Place ....

Find additional copies of this page on your CD.

About My Father

Religion

His family's religious denomination ....

Name of Congregation ....

Education

....
School Name   Place   Years Attended

....
School Name   Place   Years Attended

....
School Name   Place   Years Attended

....
School Name   Place   Years Attended

....
School Name   Place   Years Attended

Residences (not including places lived with my mother)

....
Address   Years   Description

....
Address   Years   Description

....
Address   Years   Description

....
Address   Years   Description

....
Address   Years   Description

Find additional copies of this page on your CD.

Additional Marriages (not including marriage to my mother)

Name of Spouse/Partner (include all former surnames)

....

Date of Ceremony and Place ....

If ended, date and how ....

Name of Spouse/Partner (include all former surnames)

....

Date of Ceremony and Place ....

If ended, date and how ....

Name of Spouse/Partner (include all former surnames)

....

Date of Ceremony and Place ....

If ended, date and how ....

Name of Spouse/Partner (include all former surnames)

....

Date of Ceremony and Place ....

If ended, date and how ....

My Father's Childhood Stories

Who was he named after?

How does he feel about his name?

....

....

....

....

What was he like as a child? Describe his
appearance and personality.

....

....

....

....

Describe his childhood home(s) and neighborhood(s). Tell about any place in his
home, yard, or neighborhood that was special to him.

....

....

....

Describe his upbringing: how he was raised, his financial circumstances, family
health issues, or other significant things that shaped him as a person.

....

....

....

Find additional copies of this page on your CD.

> **TIP**
>
> Insert a Memorabilia
> page with photos
> of your father at
> different ages. If your
> father is still living,
> have him complete
> this form about
> himself, if possible.

My Father: During My Childhood

Complete this form if your father was alive during your childhood. If your father is still living, have him complete this form about himself, if possible.

What was your father's daily life like while you were growing up?

(Think about his employment, parenting, volunteering, recreation, travel, etc.)

....

....

Describe his health during these years (well-being, illnesses, injuries).

....

....

What were his greatest challenges during these years?

....

....

What were his triumphs or successes during these years?

....

....

What were his most rewarding relationships during these years?
His most difficult ones?

....

....

What were your father's greatest goals or hopes during these years?
Were they realized?

....

....

Find additional copies of this page on your CD.

Me & My Father: Childhood

Describe the time you spent with your father during your childhood. What did you do together? Did you enjoy it? Did you spend enough time together?

....

....

....

....

....

....

....

....

....

....

....

....

> **TIP**
>
> Send the companion form, Me and My Child, to your father to fill out. Send Special Forms for him to document additional recollections.

How did your father show he cared about you?

....

....

....

....

....

....

Find additional copies of this page on your CD.

Me & My Father: Childhood

How did your father discipline you? What did you think about his discipline methods then? What do you think now?

....

....

....

....

....

How did your father's opinions or beliefs (religious, cultural, social, political, etc.) affect you as a child?

....

....

....

....

....

....

Write any favorite memories of yourself and your father during your childhood.

....

....

....

....

....

Find additional copies of this page on your CD.

My Parents' Relationship

If possible, have one (or both) of your parents fill out this section about themselves. Fill out additional copies for step-parents, etc.

How did your parents meet? Describe their dating life.

....

....

....

....

....

TIP

Include a photo of your parents together and/or a copy of their marriage certificate or announcement on a Memorabilia page.

Marriage

....

Date   Place

What was their wedding (or early time together) like?

....

....

....

Residences my parents shared

....

Place   Years   Description

....

Place   Years   Description

....

Place   Years   Description

Find additional copies of this page on your CD.

My Parents' Relationship

What was their relationship like? What interests and values did they share?
How were they different? How did they work out conflicts?

....

....

....

....

....

....

....

....

What did you learn from their relationship? (If a parent is filling this out:
what did you learn from your relationship that you want your child to know?)

....

....

....

....

....

....

....

If the relationship ended:

....
Date   Circumstance (death, divorce, legal separation, etc.)

Find additional copies of this page on your CD.

About My Sibling

Have each sibling complete this form, or complete it on their behalf. Find additional copies on your CD.

TIP

Insert Memorabilia pages with photos of your sibling at different ages.

Name

....
First   Middle   Last

....
Gender

....
Birth Date, Birthplace

....
Death Date   Burial Location

Parents we share

☐ Mother (if not, mother's name:)..

☐ Father (if not, father's name:)..

Raised by (if not parents):

....
Names   Relation

Education

....
School Name   Place   Years Attended

....
School Name   Place   Years Attended

....
School Name   Place   Years Attended

Find additional copies of this page on your CD.

About My Sibling

Marriages

Name of Spouse/Partner (include all former surnames)

....

Date of Ceremony, Place ....

If ended, how and when ....

Name of Spouse/Partner (include all former surnames)

....

Date of Ceremony, Place ....

If ended, how and when ....

Children

Name ....

Birth Date, Birthplace ....

Spouse ....

Death Date ....

Name ....

Birth Date, Birthplace ....

Spouse ....

Death Date ....

Name ....

Birth Date, Birthplace ....

Spouse ....

Death Date ....

Find additional copies of this page on your CD.

My Sibling's Childhood Stories

Have each sibling complete this form, or complete it on their behalf. Find additional copies on your CD.

Who were you named after?

How do you feel about your name?

TIP

Send a copy of this form to your sibling(s) to fill out.

....

....

....

....

....

....

....

What were you like as a child? Describe your appearance and personality as you remember them.

....

....

....

....

....

....

....

....

Find additional copies of this page on your CD.

Me & My Sibling During Childhood

_____

Send a copy of this form to each of your siblings, and fill it out yourself about each of them.

What was your relationship like with your sibling? Did one lead/follow, tease, bully, ignore, and/or look out for the other? Were you rivals and/or friends?

....

....

....

What did you and your sibling share: bedroom, toys, clothes, books, or the lime-light? How well did you share these?

....

....

....

Write something unique about your relationship: a special language or joke you shared, common interests, intense rivalry, etc.

....

....

....

Write any additional memories of your sibling and yourself.

....

....

....

Find additional copies of this page on your CD.

4

Stories From Childhood

Our earliest years shaped our lives and often include our fondest memories. But the older we get, the more remote our youngest years can seem. The task of transforming wispy or forgotten childhood recollections into vivid, written ones can seem daunting. This chapter will help, with a steady stream of carefully targeted questions and plenty of flexibility for your memories to flow in whatever direction they may.

Understanding Childhood Memories

Many people don't have clear, consistent memories of life before age ten. Chances are good that you're not going to recall details, but most of us do remember something. We may recall that we were generally happy. We may have sensory memories that manifest themselves as déjà vu when we smell mothballs (grandma's closet) or eat frozen custard (summers at the beach). We may have composite memories of playing in a backyard or neighborhood park over the course of many years.

It is common to have vivid memories of highly emotional or stressful childhood events: a parent's departure, surgery, the state spelling bee competition. When you start to think about your childhood, those recollections may surface first and overshadow other memories. You may need to prod yourself to look past those prominent memories to recall the details and events of everyday life. After all, a typical childhood is constructed of daily routines, not action-packed drama.

Finally, our childhood memories may not always make sense. When we stored young memories away, they were relatively raw—perhaps just images, emotional impressions, or song fragments. We didn't assign the same complex meanings to them that we would today.

Reconstructing the Distant Past

To reconstruct your earliest memories, use the same process you use to reconstruct other memories: Lay out what you remember, elaborate on it to the best of your ability, and ask others for help.

You can rely on any of the memory-jogging techniques mentioned in chapter one and try these two strategies:

1. Borrow memories from parents, siblings, or your gossipy longtime neighbor. You have to do this, to some extent. After all, you don't recall your own birth and infancy. You have likely already adopted other people's memories as your own without being aware of it. You can also borrow memories from photographs or home movies, which often offer important clues to events and personalities. When you are aware that a memory is borrowed, try to credit the source.

2. Research your own past. These days, it's possible to research almost any topic online. With Google Maps <www.maps.google.com>, you can virtually retrace the walk from your apartment to the elementary school or use the Street View function to see an image of the apartment or school (if they are still there). Look for stats on your high-school state basketball championship game. Research a family member's illness, religious or ethnic background, or another topic that affected your life, but you were too young to understand the details at the time.

Again, credit the information you find (italics, below) and try to connect it to a personal recollection: "*According to the state athletics association website,* we won the championship game by a wide margin (84–55), but all I really remember is the long ride to the game with my girlfriends, and screaming ourselves hoarse in the stands."

Special Forms Suggestions

Special People
Special Places
Special Memories
Life-Changing
Experiences
Flashbulb Memories
Memorabilia
More
In Memoriam

On Your CD
My Pet
My Home
Me & My Child (for
your parent to complete)
Homeschooling (use in
combination with or
instead of traditional
school forms)
Summer Camp
Travel Log

My Birth

Additional details about your birth are requested in chapter two.

....
Birth Date (Day, Month, Year)

....
Birthplace

What were the circumstances of your parents' lives before your birth or adoption?

....

....

....

....

....

....

TIP

Send a parent or older sibling a More page with a request for stories about your infant and toddler years. If your parent kept a baby book for you, look for answers there.

What have you been told about your birth (including who was there or who should have been, labor or delivery complications, your appearance or health at birth, your parents' feelings)?

....

....

....

....

....

....

....

My Birth

Why were you named as you were? How did you feel about your name when you were young? What about now?

....

....

....

....

What do you know about your early health and physical development (teething, talking, walking, eating, and social behavior)?

....

....

....

....

Write down stories you have been told about yourself as a baby or toddler, including those about your relationships with siblings, parents, or others.

....

....

....

....

....

....

....

....

....

Childhood Personality

Describe your personality as a child: shy, friendly, outgoing, nervous, energetic, obedient, willful, funny, charming, competitive. Share any memories that show your personality.

....

....

....

....

....

....

....

....

....

....

....

TIP

Just for fun, send copies of this form to your parent(s) and/or sibling(s) to fill out about you. See how your memories and opinions are similar and different.

Who influenced your tastes and interests most during your childhood?

....

....

....

....

....

....

Find additional copies of this page on your CD.

Childhood Personality

What did you really like to do as a child (crafts, games, electronics, art, build or invent things, music, visit museums, sports, write, play outside, be with friends)?

....

....

....

....

....

....

....

....

....

....

....

....

....

....

....

....

....

....

....

....

Find additional copies of this page on your CD.

Home

....

When did you live here?

....

TIP

Include a Memorabilia page with photos of your home or neighborhood.

Describe your home. Think about the layout, size, décor, comfort level, and special details or rooms you liked or disliked.

....

....

....

....

....

....

Describe any improvements you and/or your family made to your home or yard. What difference did these improvements make?

....

....

....

....

....

....

....

Find additional copies of this page on your CD.

Home

Where did you spend most of your time when you were at home?
What did you do there?

....

....

....

....

....

....

Write about your yard and/or neighborhood. Was it busy, peaceful, loud, dangerous, grassy, friendly, fun, huge, boring?

....

....

....

....

....

....

Who did you interact with in your neighborhood?

....

....

....

....

Find additional copies of this page on your CD.

Everyday Life

Before you started school, who took care of you? Who else was with you? What kinds of things did you do? Share a memory (even a fragment or a borrowed memory) from your preschool years.

....

....

....

TIP

Document travel on a Travel Log or Special Memories form. If you attended summer camp, document it on the Summer Camp form on your CD.

As a schoolchild, what was your after-school routine like? Who took care of you?

....

....

....

....

What did you do on weekends or other days off? Who was with you?

....

....

....

What did you do during the summer? Who took care of you?

....

....

....

....

Everyday Life

Did you like to be at home? Why or why not?

....

....

....

....

What kinds of foods did your family eat? Describe mealtimes, favorite foods, who prepared meals, etc. What were your favorite (and least favorite) foods?

....

....

....

....

What kinds of chores did you do? Did you help take care of siblings or other youngsters?

....

....

....

....

Was your home clean, cluttered, or chaotic? Who took charge of neatness?

....

....

....

....

Everyday Life

For what were you punished as a child, and how were you punished?

....

....

....

....

What did you do for fun at home? Who did you play with?
Share a playtime memory.

....

....

....

....

Describe any favorite toys. Why did you love them? Share a memory about toys.

....

....

....

....

What television shows or radio programs did your family enjoy?
Did you have a favorite?

....

....

....

....

Everyday Life

What did you read for fun when you were young?
Did anyone read with you?

....
....
....

TIP

Print an extra copy of
the My Pet form from
your CD to honor and
record details about
pets you really loved.

Did you go to the movies or the theater as a child?
Share memories of a favorite show or a fun time out.

....
....
....

What did you wear most days and on special occasions?
Describe any clothes you loved or hated.

....
....
....

Describe pets your family had. How did you feel about them?
Who took care of them?

....
....
....
....
....

My Childhood Health

Describe any medical conditions you had when you were born. What measures were taken to correct or manage those conditions?

....

....

....

....

....

....

....

Were you immunized? ☐ Yes ☐ No ☐ Not sure

Were you breast-fed? ☐ Yes ☐ No ☐ Not sure

Were you colicky? ☐ Yes ☐ No ☐ Not sure

TIP

If you don't know these answers, ask someone. Attach a Memorabilia page with a copy of your immunization record, an allergy or hospital ID bracelet, or other evidence of your physical health and well-being in your younger years.

Describe what you know of your health as an infant and toddler. Include things like allergies, frequent ear infections or colds, asthma, or delays in normal physical development (like walking and talking).

....

....

....

....

....

....

....

My Childhood Health

....
....
....
....
....
....

What about your health during your elementary and middle school years?
Did you have any broken bones or teeth, surgery, or physical or speech therapy?
Did you wear glasses or braces? Write any memories of being physically
able-bodied or restricted.

....
....
....
....
....
....
....
....
....
....
....
....
....

Childhood Companions

Describe your earliest childhood playmates
and friends from school. What were they like?
What did you do together?

....

....

....

....

....

....

....

....

....

....

....

TIP

Include a Special
People form for
particularly close
friends. Send Special
Memories forms to
childhood friends, or
use them yourself to
describe a particularly
memorable
experience with a
friend.

Tell about any childhood "enemies": a bully; an athletic, academic, or social rival;
or a grown-up or kid who just seemed to have it in for you.

....

....

....

....

....

....

....

Childhood Companions

....
....
....
....
....
....

Write about time spent with family friends (your parents' friends).
What kinds of things did you all do together? What other children were there?
Did you enjoy this time?

....
....
....
....
....
....
....
....
....
....
....
....
....
....
....

Elementary School Days

What is your earliest memory of elementary school?

....

....

....

Write about any traditions you and your family observed at the beginning of the school year.

....

....

....

For names and locations of schools attended, see chapter two. Find forms on homeschooling on your CD; use them instead of or in combination with this page, which is geared toward a bricks-and-mortar school environment.

List any elementary teachers you recall. What do you remember about them?

....

....

....

How did you feel about school? In what subjects did you perform well? Poorly?

....

....

Describe a time when you were teased by or embarrassed in front of your peers. How did you react? What do you think about that now?

....

....

Elementary School Days

What did you eat for lunch at school? Describe your lunchtime.

....

....

....

What were your favorite activities during recess?

....

....

Describe any special elementary school activities or honors: student of the
month, orchestra, school play, crossing guard, teacher's helper, spelling bee,
math competition, or a compliment from a teacher.

....

....

....

Did you ever get in trouble, or were you sent to the principal's office? What for?

....

....

Think about activities you did outside of school—Scouts, 4-H, music lessons,
karate class, etc. Write memories of your participation (age, name of organization,
leaders or friends, and what your participation meant to you).

....

....

Middle Grades

For names and locations of schools attended, see chapter two.
Find a form on homeschooling on your CD.

How did your school life change when you reached middle or junior high school?

....

....

Describe your social life and friendships during junior high school.

....

....

Describe a time when you were teased or embarrassed in front of your peers.
How did you react? What do you think about that experience now?

....

....

List any middle-grade teachers you recall. Describe any memories of them.

....

....

How did you feel about going to school each day? How well did you do in
different subjects?

....

....

Tell about any extra activities you were involved with during these years (sports,
clubs, etc.) What did it mean to you to be involved in these?

....

....

Middle Grades

Describe any special honors or compliments you recall receiving during junior high or middle school years. What did you think of these at the time?

....

....

....

TIP

Document travel on a Travel Log or Special Memories form. If you attended summer camp, document it on the Summer Camp form on your CD.

Write about a disappointment you recall in school: doing unexpectedly poorly on a test or project, losing a student election, not placing in a competition, etc. How do you feel about that experience now?

....

....

....

Did you ever get in trouble? What for? ....

....

How do you feel now about your overall experience in middle or junior high school?

....

....

What did you do during school vacations in the spring, summer, and winter (as well as any other breaks you had)? ....

....

Childhood Celebrations & Traditions

How did your family celebrate your birthday when you were young?
Were there parties? Who came? What were your favorite gifts?
Was your birthday ever a disappointment?

....

....

....

How did your family (or your parents, if you weren't invited) celebrate the
New Year when you were a child? Write about the first time you recall staying
up until midnight. ....

....

....

What holidays or traditions did your family observe during the spring?

....

....

....

....

....

Write your memories of national or patriotic celebrations. Where did you
celebrate, how, and with whom? How did you feel about them?

....

....

....

Childhood Celebrations & Traditions

How did your family celebrate Halloween? Tell about any favorite costumes, parties, decorations, food, where you trick-or-treated, haunted house tours, etc.

....
....
....

How did you celebrate Thanksgiving or other fall celebrations. Where did you gather? Who cooked and baked? Write about the tastes, smells, and other sensory memories.

....
....
....

What winter holidays did your family celebrate? Write about a typical holiday observance: decorations, music, food, gift-giving, religious rituals, and family traditions.

....
....
....

What additional holidays did your family observe? Describe your traditions.

....
....
....
....

5

Stories From High School

Whether you came of age in the 1940s or 1990s, your teen years were likely full of "firsts": first job, first date, first time behind the wheel. You made decisions about college, career, perhaps even marriage and childbearing. However, you may still have kept one foot in childhood, refusing to surrender beloved toys or rituals even as you started shaving.

Your high school years are likely a mixed bag of memories. You may recall some poignant coming-of-age tales; power struggles with your parents; and made-for-movie moments in which you scored gloriously (on or off the field). You've also probably got memories of everyday life in which you went to school, faced down finals, and hoped you'd have something exciting to do on Friday night.

As with childhood memories, dramatic memories may overshadow everyday ones. In this chapter, you will record both. The memory prompts will hit the highlights and also the stories and relationships of everyday life.

Some people are wary of facing their teenage selves, with memories of social awkwardness, bad decisions, or long-buried pain over things that went wrong. In this chapter, you can record some of those things if you like, but you will also look at the positives: your friendships, kindnesses, and good choices.

Of course, you don't need to write about every detail of your teen years. But do record your current feelings about past experiences whenever you can. Today's perspective is part of the process of telling your story. Anything you learned, any sense of humor or compassion you show toward your younger self—these are valuable both to yourself and to your readers.

Research Is Actually Fun

Researching your teen years is way more fun than it sounds. If you left a paper trail of any kind—letters or notes, diaries, yearbooks—read them. You may find yourself charmed by your sense of humor, or feeling a new compassion for this young kid who was just trying to navigate high school halls without mishap. In yearbook entries, you may find evidence of friendships, hopeless crushes, inside jokes, and other social drama long forgotten.

Indulge yourself in the sights, sounds, and scenes of the past. Listen to old Top 40 albums. Try on your old letter jacket. Tour a vintage car show; if you're at least forty, you'll probably find your favorite rides on display. Attend a high school football game or wander the mall and study the younger crowd. Watch a defining movie of that age, whether it was *Rebel Without a Cause, The Graduate,* or *The Breakfast Club.* Jog your memories of fads and fashions by flipping through lifestyle magazines from your teen years or the *This Fabulous Century* series (Time-Life Books) (find these at libraries).

Connecting with old friends can spark a lot of memories and offer opportunities for others to participate in your book. Get in touch with a high school buddy, teacher, or coach. Refer to the section "Enlisting Help" in chapter one for tips on collecting memories from friends and teachers.

Family Life Continues

We don't often think of family life as an important part of the teenage experience. But the folks at home still influenced you, even if you spent most of your time at school, work, friends' houses, or the alley behind the five-and-dime.

You'll write about your relationships with your parents and siblings. In other words, you can give credit where it is due—with a family member who worked hard to care for you—and/or explain family challenges you faced at a young age.

Special Pages Suggestions

Special People
Special Places
Special Memories
Life-Changing Experiences
Flashbulb Memories
Memorabilia
More
In Memoriam

On Your CD

My Pet
My Home
Jobs
Me & My Teenager (for
your parents to complete)
Homeschooling (use in
combination with or
instead of traditional
school forms)
Summer Camp
Travel Log

Teenage Personality

How would you describe your personality as a teenager? How did you act around others your age, your family, and at school?

....

....

....

How did you respond to new challenges or situations?

....

....

....

TIP

Just for fun, send copies of this form to your parent(s) and/or sibling(s) to fill out about you. See how your memories and opinions are similar and different.

What did you think of yourself at this age? Were you confident, critical, or accepting of yourself? What do you think about your teenage self now?

....

....

....

What did you like to do on your own: daydream, read, listen to the radio, watch television, work on hobbies or collections, play sports, or wander your neighborhood?

....

....

....

Find additional copies of this page on your CD.

Teenage Personality

What were you good at as a teenager? Think about all kinds of gifts, talents, or interests: social, musical, athletic, artistic, leadership, academic, inventive, compassionate, etc.

....

....

....

What did you believe about right and wrong, religion, and the like? Whose values, opinions, or actions influenced your beliefs most during these years?

....

....

....

....

....

....

Tell about a time (or more than one time) when you were kind to someone or did a good deed.

....

....

Tell about a time when you were mean or unkind to someone.

....

....

Find additional copies of this page on your CD.

Health and Well-Being

How healthy were you as a teenager? How did your health or any injuries affect your daily life at home, at school, and with friends?

....

....

....

....

....

TIP

If you don't know the answers for this page, ask someone. Attach a Memorabilia page with a copy of a doctor's chart, hospital ID bracelet, or related mementoes.

Think about your physical growth and changes as a teenager: acne, being the tallest or shortest, "getting your figure," etc. How did these changes affect you?

....

....

....

....

Describe your emotional health as a teenager: Were you happy, anxious, nervous, depressed, angry, aggressive, low-key, content, moody? How did you and your family handle any emotional difficulties you experienced?

....

....

....

....

....

Tough Teenage Choices

Feel free to remove this form if you prefer not to answer these questions—
or add a blank continuation page and tell lots of stories!

What were common attitudes among your friends toward teenage drinking,
smoking, drug use, or reckless or illegal behavior?

....
....
....
....

How did your parents feel about these activities? What motivations did they give
you for avoiding them?

....
....
....
....

Write about your choices regarding teenage drinking, smoking, drug use,
or reckless or illegal behavior. What motivated you? What were your
experiences like? What consequences did you face? What impact did your
choices have on your life?

....
....
....
....
....

Planning for the Future

As a teen, how did you feel about the future: excited or afraid?
Or did you ignore the future altogether?

....
....
....
....
....
....

What did you want to do when you grew up?
How passionate were you about your plans?

....
....
....
....
....
....

How did your plans for the future shape the choices you made in high school?

....
....
....
....
....

Planning for the Future

How did your circumstances as a teen affect your hopes for the future?
Consider things like money, access to education, romantic ties,
and obligations to loved ones.

....

....

....

....

....

How did others' attitudes affect your hopes for the future?
Did your parents have strong feelings about what they wanted you to do?

....

....

....

....

....

What did you want to do when you finished high school—and what did
you actually do? Why? What do you think of those choices today?

....

....

....

....

....

Home Life

What were your responsibilities at home during your teen years?
Describe any chores you had. Did you do your own cooking, laundry, tidying, etc.?

....

....

....

....

....

....

Did you receive an allowance or spending money? If so, did you have to earn it,
and what did you do with it? How did this affect you, both then and now?

....

....

....

....

Describe your home environment during your teenage years: peaceful,
(un)comfortable, (un)predictable, (un)happy, (in)tolerant, (un)welcoming,
boring? Did you enjoy being at home? Did your friends like to come over?

....

....

....

....

....

Home Life

How did your parents treat you when you were a teenager?
Were they interested in your thoughts and feelings?
How did they discipline you? How much did they trust you?

....

....

....

....

....

If you had siblings, did your parents treat you and your siblings pretty much the
same, or were there differences? How did you feel about this at the time? What
do you think about it now?

....

....

....

....

....

Looking back, how do you think your home life influenced your decisions and
friendships as a teenager?

....

....

....

....

Me & My Mother: Teen Years

Describe your relationship with your mother during
your teen years. What did you do together?

....

....

....

....

....

....

....

....

....

TIP

Fill out another copy
for a step-mom. Send
the companion form
Me and My Teenager
to your mother to fill
out about you (find
it on your CD). Send
her Special Memories
or More forms to
request additional
recollections.

What did you agree or disagree about? How did you work out conflict?

....

....

....

....

....

....

....

....

....

Find additional copies of this page on your CD.

Me & My Mother: Teen Years

How did your mother support you during these years? Consider employment, sacrifices made, time spent together, help with homework, listening, offering advice, etc. If your mother was not supportive, write about that.

....

....

....

....

....

....

....

....

....

Write any special memories of you and your mother from your teen years.

....

....

....

....

....

....

....

....

....

Find additional copies of this page on your CD.

Me & My Father: Teen Years

Describe your relationship with your father during your teen years. What did you do together?

....

....

....

....

....

....

....

....

....

....

TIP

Fill out another copy for a step-dad. Send the companion form Me and My Teenager to your father to fill out about you (find it on your CD). Send him Special Memories or More forms to request additional recollections.

What did you agree or disagree about? How did you work out conflict?

....

....

....

....

....

....

....

....

....

Find additional copies of this page on your CD.

Me & My Father: Teen Years

How did your father support you during these years? Consider employment, sacrifices made, time spent together, help with homework, listening, offering advice, etc. If your father was not supportive, write about that.

....

....

....

....

....

....

....

....

....

Write any special memories of you and your father from your teen years.

....

....

....

....

....

....

....

....

....

Find additional copies of this page on your CD.

Me & My Sibling: Teen Years

TIP

Send a copy of this form to your sibling(s) to fill out.

....

Sibling's Name

How would you describe your relationship with your sibling during your teen years?

....
....
....
....
....
....

What kinds of things did you do together? What did you talk about?

....
....
....
....
....

What interests or attitudes did you and your siblings share?

....
....
....
....

Find additional copies of this page on your CD.

Me & My Sibling: Teen Years

What did you disagree or fight about? How did you work out conflict?

....

....

....

....

....

Tell about a time your sibling showed you special attention, love, or consideration, and/or a time you did that for him or her.

....

....

....

....

....

....

Write about any more special memories of you and your sibling during your teen years.

....

....

....

....

....

Find additional copies of this page on your CD.

High School Days

For names and locations of schools attended, see chapter two. Find forms on homeschooling on your CD; use them instead of or in combination with these.

Describe your high school campus and the student body: size, social/ethnic backgrounds, values, educational ambitions. How did you fit in?

....

....

....

List any memorable high school teachers, counselors, or coaches.
What made them memorable? How did they treat or influence you?

....

....

....

How did you feel about going to school each day? How did you do academically?

....

....

....

Were you ever recognized for special talents or achievements? How? Did you receive compliments, awards, honors, or leadership or other opportunities?

....

....

....

High School Days

Write about a time when you were disappointed in your performance (as a student, athlete, or in another area). How do you feel about that experience now?

....
....
....

TIP

Use a Travel Log form for frequent travel. Document camp experiences on the Summer Camp form on your CD.

Did you ever get in trouble at school? What for?

....
....
....

If you graduated, write about your high school graduation. If you didn't graduate, write about why not, or what you were doing instead.

....
....
....
....

What did you do during school vacations in the spring, summer, and winter (as well as any other breaks you had)?

....
....
....
....

Friends

Who were your closest friends when you were a teenager? Describe them. How did you get to be friends? What did you do together? How did you feel about them?

....

....

....

Write about your larger circle of friends, if you had one. What did you have in common? How loyal were you to each other?

....

....

....

TIP

Fill out a Special People form for close friends. Use a Special Memories page to describe a particularly memorable experience with a friend. Send Special Memories forms to friends from high school to request their thoughts of your time together.

Did you ever argue or fight with a good friend? Who? What happened? How did it end?

....

....

....

Where did you hang out with friends? A restaurant, shopping center, park, or other location? Why? Describe it.

....

....

Friends

Who were your rivals at school, on the sports field, or in your social life?
Write about your conflicts and how they went.

....

....

....

Did you ever take any social risks, like befriending a less-popular kid, standing
up for an unpopular cause, or treating a popular kid badly? Tell what happened.
Was it worth it?

....

....

....

Tell about a time you were teased or embarrassed in front of your peers.
How did you react? What do you think about that now?

....

....

....

In what way(s) did you stand out from the crowd as a teenager: looks, abilities,
race, religion, personal interests, gender, attitudes, or culture? How did this affect
your social life and your sense of yourself?

....

....

....

Romance

Describe any school or community dances you attended. Did you enjoy them? Who did you dance with? What kind of music or dancing was there? What did you wear? Don't forget Homecoming, prom, or Sadie Hawkins (girls' choice) dances.

....
....
....
....
....
....
....

Tell about your first romance or crush.
What attracted you? How did the relationship go?

....
....
....
....
....
....
....
....

Romance

How interested were you in dating, and what was your dating life like?
Name any serious boy/girlfriends, and describe your relationship(s).

....

....

....

....

....

How did you learn about "the birds and the bees"?

....

....

....

....

....

Share any thoughts on teenage romance. What lessons did you learn about
love (and/or sexuality) during your teenage years? What advice would you give
young people today on this topic?

....

....

....

....

....

Fashions

What were clothing fashions like when you were a teenager? Think about colors, shoes/boots, and accessories like jewelry, hats, scarves, and sunglasses. Who were famous fashion icons at the time?

....

....

....

How did you typically dress during your teenage years? Did you like the way you dressed? Why did you dress this way?

....

....

....

TIP

Look through old photos and your yearbooks to remind yourself of high school fashions. The beginning of this chapter lists other resources that can remind you about fads and fashions. Add Memorabilia pages with images of the fads and fashions you write about.

Describe a favorite outfit.

....

....

....

How did you style your hair as a teenager? How did this style compare to those of your peers? Did you like your hairstyle?

....

....

....

Fads

What kind of music was popular during your teen years?
What did you think of it?

....

....

What music did *you* listen to as a teenager?
Who influenced your tastes? Write a memory
connected to popular music.

TIP

See the resources
referenced at the
beginning of this
chapter for more on
fads and fashions.
Add Memorabilia
pages with images of
the fads and fashions
you write about.

....

....

....

What books, magazines, television shows, and movies do you recall from your
teen years? Which were popular among your friends? Did any strongly influence
the way you thought or acted?

....

....

Who were the popular heroes and celebrities of your teen years?
Who were your favorites? Any teen idol crushes or favorite females?

....

....

Write any sayings or phrases that were popular during your teenage years.
(Think how you described something great—as "groovy" or "the bee's knees"—
or an attractive person—"hot mama" or "hipster.")

....

....

Extracurricular Activities

What extracurricular activities did you do at school: sports teams, clubs, organizations, ensembles, social groups, productions, etc.?

....

....

....

....

....

....

> **TIP**
>
> Attach team photos, newspaper clippings, or programs to Memorabilia pages.

What activities, clubs, or sports did you participate in outside of school: community, church, social, or service groups, teams, programs, or activities?

....

....

....

....

....

Why did you participate in these activities?

....

....

....

....

....

Extracurricular Activities

Describe your experience with these activities. If it was competitive, how often did you practice? How long was the season? Did your team have a winning record? If it was a club, how often did you meet? What did you do?

....
....
....
....
....
....

What did you learn from participating in these activities?

....
....
....
....
....

Describe a time you really shined during an extracurricular activity.

....
....
....
....
....

First Job

What was your first paying job? Who did you work for?
What did you do?

TIP

Use additional Jobs forms on your CD to write about other jobs you had in high school.

....

....

....

....

....

How old were you when you started this job?

....

How much were you paid?.......................................

How did you get the job?

....

....

....

Why did you work?

....

....

....

....

....

....

First Job

How did you feel on your first day?

....
....
....
....
....

What did you learn by working?

....
....
....
....
....

What did you do with the money you earned?

....
....
....

Why did you stop doing this job?

....
....
....

Behind the Wheel

Who taught you how to drive? Describe any difficulties, fears, or mishaps that happened. If you never learned to drive, explain why.

TIP

Attach a photo of your first car to a Memorabilia page.

....

....

....

....

....

How old were you when you got your driver's license, and how did you feel when you got it?

....

....

....

....

....

Did you have a car? If so, how did you get it? Describe any cars you drove—make, model, year, color, and distinctive features, including any nickname you gave it.

....

....

....

....

....

Behind the Wheel

How often did you drive, and where did you drive to? If you didn't drive, how did you get from place to place?

....

....

....

....

....

....

....

....

....

What was your dream car as a teenager? Did anyone you knew have a great car? If so, describe it.

....

....

....

....

....

....

....

....

....

6

Stories From My Professional Life

"What do you do?"

It's the first question many people in the United States ask when they meet someone socially. Why? Because "what you do," why you do it, how you feel about it, and the relationships you create tell a lot about your character, values, interests, skills or talents, family or social culture, and endurance. This applies whether you have a high-paying job or not. In fact, sometimes, it's those with lower-paying (or nonpaying) work whose jobs reveal the most or the best about them.

For the purposes of this chapter, your "work" might include any combination of advanced education, paid employment, unpaid work around the house, military commitments, and volunteer service. You'll capture the different aspects of your daily work from young adulthood to retirement.

You will likely find yourself rearranging or removing a section or two in this chapter; after all, most people haven't done everything! (If you have, congratulations! You have a lot to write about.) But you might find yourself adding things, too. If you've had a lot of work experience or re-enlisted in the military, you'll want to print some extra forms from your CD.

In this professional life chapter, questions about relationships revolve around people you have known as college buddies, coworkers, professors, bosses, fellow volunteers, etc. (Romance and family relationships are covered separately, in chapter eight.) The exception will be questions about how your professional life (and that of your partner) affected your personal and family life over the years. If your professional and personal life have been intertwined (your true love worked in the next cubicle over, or you were part of a family business), consider adding extra pages to describe how that worked out.

There is a special section on page 125 called "Work in the Home" that focuses on the unpaid work of managing a household. It can be surprisingly satisfying to describe the work you've done at home, which is often underappreciated. Even if you were never the primary "homemaker" in your home, you likely shared responsibility for some chores, and you deserve a chance to document it. If your daily work included caring for children and/or a partner you, you will have the opportunity to write more about that in chapter seven, Stories About a Family of Your Own.

You may have to dig deep into your memory to recall details about early employment, college years, and the like. Consider writing to former employers to request copies of your personnel files. Give yourself plenty of time to reminisce both alone and with others who can help you remember. Be patient: It's worth the effort, particularly to your readers, who want to know about your formative young-adult years. The decisions you made during that time and the lessons you learned are some of the most important you can pass along.

College

What colleges, technical schools, etc., did you apply to?
Why did you apply there?

....
....
....
....
....
....
....
....
....

TIP

Find more details in chapter one about schools attended. If you attended multiple colleges (including military academy), you may want to print additional College forms from your CD.

Where did you attend school? How did you feel about going there?

....
....
....
....
....
....
....
....
....
....

College

What did your family think about you going to school? Was it expected?
Was anyone particularly proud, jealous, excited, angry, or sad about you going?

....

....

....

....

....

....

What concerns did your parents express about you going to school: money,
grades, homesickness, social life, etc.? How did they show their concern?

....

....

....

....

....

....

What concerned you the most about going to college: money, grades,
homesickness, social life, etc?

....

....

....

....

....

....

Academic Life

What course of study did you choose and why?
Tell if you changed your major(s), and why.

....
....
....
....
....
....
....
....

How well did you do in school overall? What classes did you most enjoy?
Least enjoy? Did you attend classes regularly, or skip them?

....
....
....
....
....

Describe your study habits. Did you study a lot or a little? Alone or with a group?

....
....
....
....
....

Academic Life

Think of a time you worked especially hard on a class assignment.
What was it? How did it go?

....
....
....
....
....
....

Think of a time you ignored an important assignment or waited until the last
minute. What were the results?

....
....
....
....
....
....

Write about a professor, tutor, or another mentor who made a difference in
your college life.

....
....
....
....

Campus Life

Describe your school campus: size, location, urban/ rural, etc. Was there a spot on campus you particularly liked or avoided?

....
....
....
....

Did you pledge a sorority or fraternity? Why or why not?

....
....
....

Where did you live while you were at school? What was it like? What did you eat?

....
....
....

Who did you live with at school? How did they influence your experience?

....
....
....
....

Campus Life

What did you do—or where did you go—when you needed a break from campus life? Describe a favorite memory of a getaway.

....

....

....

....

....

....

....

If you lived at home (or visited during school breaks), how did your relationship with your parents/siblings change? Did you still have to obey "house rules" about curfews, chores, etc.? How did you feel about that?

....

....

....

....

....

What was your school vacation schedule?
What did you usually do during breaks?

....

....

....

....

Extracurricular Activities

What extracurricular activities did you participate in while in college? Describe sports teams (intramural or through your school), clubs, organizations, ensembles, social groups, productions, etc.

....
....
....
....
....
....
....

Why did you participate in these activities?

....
....
....
....
....

Describe your experience with these activities. If it was competitive, how often did you practice? How long was the season? Did your team have a winning record? If it was a club, how often did you meet? What did you do?

....
....
....
....

Extracurricular Activities

What role, if any, did political or cultural activism play in your daily life and/or major decisions during your college years?

....
....
....
....
....
....
....
....
....

What role, if any, did religion play in your daily life and/or major decisions during your college years?

....
....
....
....
....
....
....
....
....

Social Life

Who were your best friends at school? How did you meet?
What did you like about each other?

....
....
....
....

Was there a particular group of friends you associated with, like those
who participated in arts, sports, Greek life, or those with shared culture,
race, or politics?

....
....
....
....

What were your biggest social pressures as a student?
How did you handle them?

....
....
....
....

Describe a time or place you felt very alone or out of your comfort zone.

....
....
....

Graduation

Describe your college graduation. If you did not graduate, write about why not, or what you were doing instead.

TIP

Add a Memorabilia page with a copy of your diploma and/or graduation photos.

....

....

....

....

....

....

What did you want to do right after college—and what did you actually do? Why? What do you think of those choices today?

....

....

....

....

....

....

Did you ever go back to school (attend graduate school, continuing education, etc)? Why or why not?

....

....

....

....

....

....

Work Life

Describe your first full-time job. How old were you when you started?
How long did it take you to find a full-time job?

....
....
....
....
....
....

What were your hopes and expectations for your working life?
Did you plan to make a lot of money quickly, grow in a career path over time,
or stay at the same job until retirement?

....
....
....
....
....

How did you feel during your first six months to a year of full-time work?
What did you learn about yourself and about your job?

....
....
....
....
....
....

Work Life

If you switched jobs a lot, how did you feel about that? Did you like these changes or were they hard on you? Why?

....

....

....

....

....

If you have not yet retired, what are your goals or hopes for your future career?

....

....

....

....

If you have not yet retired, what are your concerns about your future career?

....

....

....

....

....

....

....

....

Jobs

....
Employer name

....
Employer location

....
Date(s) employed

....
How much were you paid?

....
What was your schedule (hours per week)?

Why did you want this job?

....
....

How did you get this job? (How did you find out about it?
Who helped or recommended you? What was your interview like?
How did you feel when you got it?)

....
....
....

What skills, techniques, or knowledge did you have to learn on the job in
order to succeed? Who taught you?

....
....

Find additional copies of this page on your CD.

> **TIP**
>
> Print as many of
> these forms as you
> need to cover your full
> paid work history.

Jobs

How well did you do at this job? Think about your skills, productivity, working well with others, following orders or instructions, etc.

....
....
....
....

Why did you stop working here? How did you feel about leaving?

....
....
....

What life lessons did you learn at this job? What about other benefits, like friends made or skills learned?

....
....
....
....

What effect, if any, did this job have on your personal or family life?

....
....
....
....

Find additional copies of this page on your CD.

Work in the Home

This section captures the unpaid work of managing a household. These questions apply to most everyone, whether you were a "homemaker" or not.

Who managed your household during your adult life? If it changed over the years, how did it change?

....

....

What were your household duties? (Cooking, cleaning, clothing care, shopping, gardening/yard work, preserving food, caring for livestock or pets, household repairs, auto maintenance, taking out the trash, arranging for repairs, etc.)

....

....

If others lived in your home, what household chores did they do?

....

....

How did you feel about your household responsibilities? If there was a division of labor between you and a partner, how did you feel about that division?

....

....

Write about something you did around the house that you were proud of. Did you remodel or decorate? Fix or organize something?

....

....

Work in the Home

For what labor-saving household devices have you been most grateful? Why?

....

....

What chores do you like the least?

....

....

What chores do you enjoy, or what chores don't bother you so much?

....

....

Describe how you managed household finances (your role/your partner's role, how you kept track of expenses, how spending decisions were made). How well did you manage your finances?

....

....

Looking back, what did you do well in handling your household responsibilities?

....

....

....

What do you wish you'd done better in your household responsibilities?

....

....

....

....

Retirement

Why did you retire when you did?

....

....

....

How did you feel about retiring?

....

....

....

How was your retirement celebrated or honored (by yourself or others)?

....

....

....

What did you do immediately after you retired?

....

....

....

How well did you adjust to retirement? How long did it take you to adjust?

....

....

If you had a partner at the time you retired, how did your partner feel about your retirement? What changes, if any, occurred in your relationship?

....

....

....

Retirement

How did your financial health change after retirement? What adjustments, if any, did you make to your lifestyle? ....

....

....

What changes, if any, did you have in friends when you retired?
Did you make new ones or spend more time with those you already had?

....

....

If you returned to paid employment after you officially retired, why?

....

....

What activities have you enjoyed since retiring that you didn't do (or do as much) when you were working?

....

....

Today, what do you enjoy about being retired?

....

....

What do you miss about working, if anything?

....

....

....

....

Military

For more details about military service, see chapter two. Consider writing about combat or other intense military experiences on a Life-Changing Experience form.

How did you decide to join the military, or were you drafted? What were you feeling when you joined?

....

....

What did your parents and/or other loved ones think about you joining the military? ....

....

....

....

How did you decide which branch of the military to join?

....

....

Describe your experience as a trainee (boot camp, ROTC, etc). What did you think of it? (If you attended a military academy, describe this experience in the College and Academic Life forms on page 111–114.)

....

....

....

Who were your friends during your military service? Why did you get along?

....

....

Military

What did you think of your commanding officer(s)?

....

....

Write about where you were stationed. What did you like or dislike about the base(s) or location(s)?

....

....

....

....

What were your daily job responsibilities? What did you think of them?

....

....

....

What did you do when you were off duty?

....

....

....

How did active duty affect your family and/or romantic relationships? Who did you miss the most? Who missed you?

....

....

....

Military

Write about a time you were commended for your work.

....

....

Write about a time you were disciplined, if you ever were.

....

....

....

....

Were you ever deployed? How did you feel about being deployed or
not being deployed?...

....

....

....

If you were deployed, describe your assignment(s). What did you do during
this time?...

....

....

....

What security clearance did you have, if any? What did you think of having
(or not having) clearance?...

....

....

....

Military

Write about a time you were in harm's way, if you ever were. What happened? Where were you? How did that experience change you? (Consider writing about combat on a Life-Changing Experiences form.)

....

....

How did others treat you as a soldier, officer, or nurse, etc? Do you feel you were treated differently in the military because of your gender, race, religion, etc?

....

....

Think of someone you admired or respected during your time in the military: an officer, soldier, political figure, relative, etc. Why did you admire that person?

....

....

How did you feel when you completed your military service?

....

....

What lessons did you learn from serving in the military?

....

....

How do you feel today about the country, ideals, or people you served?

....

....

....

Volunteer

....
Name of organization

....
Branch/location

....
Dates of service

....
Position(s) held

Why did you volunteer here?

....

....

....

TIP

For immersion volunteer experiences like the Peace Corps or traveling missionary service, consider filling out Special Memories or Life-Changing Experience forms.

What type of service did you perform? Describe the amount of time, the type of work, etc. ....

....

....

....

Write about a time that volunteering was hard or you had to give more than you expected. What was the result?

....

....

....

Find additional copies of this page on your CD.

Volunteer

Describe someone you met through volunteering whom you came to respect or admire. What did you admire about or learn from that person?

....

....

....

....

Write about a time you had fun or otherwise enjoyed your volunteer work.

....

....

....

....

How did volunteering change you? What rewards did you feel personally from it?

....

....

....

....

Why did you stop volunteering, if you stopped?

....

....

....

....

Find additional copies of this page on your CD.

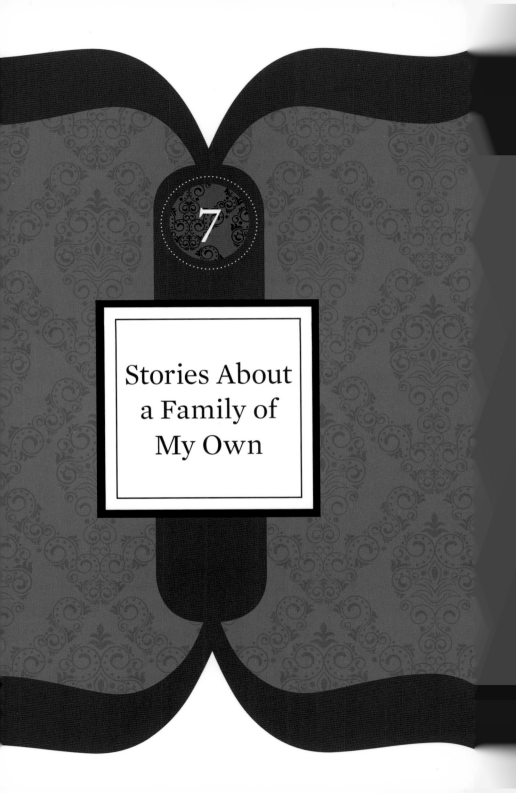

7

Stories About a Family of My Own

In this chapter you will write about the family life you've lived in adulthood. Here you can celebrate your closest family relationships. You might write about the moment you realized how much your partner loved you, those late nights cuddling your newborn son, or your joy in your daughter's (or granddaughter's) successes.

Don't skimp on this section. The people most likely to read this book are your own family members. Think how much it will mean to them to read that they have mattered in your life! Your sincere written appreciation, love, and shared memories can especially nurture vulnerable or rocky relationships, or those that have cooled over time.

You may want to try some of the memory-jogging tricks in chapter one to bring more memories to life. If you find yourself unsure of what to write regarding a parent, sibling, etc., consider using your favorite pictures of them as a starting point. Put the pictures on a Memorabilia insert. Write captions explaining why you love each picture. Does it capture something special about that person's character? Was it taken at an event you remember fondly? The process of thinking about the person may help you express what has been special about the individual or unique about your relationship.

You probably know plenty of truly embarrassing stories about your family, but think twice about telling them all. Similarly, where important family memories involve secrets, consider whether these are your secrets to share, or seek permission from someone who would be affected by your sharing them. Choose tactful and sensitive

TIPS

» Include forms about all parents and siblings who have been a part of your adult life. (Print extra copies from your CD.)

» Each "Partner" and "Child" section has multiple pages. If you and a partner or child didn't build a lasting relationship, you might remove pages that ask you to describe your relationship in detail. Wedding pages can be removed if you were not married, or may be used to describe a commitment ceremony or similar event.

» Rearrange pages in this section (or place them in other sections of the book) to fit your own timeline.

» Create Special People pages for extended relatives

ways to share feelings or memories that might cause a loved one pain. Consider using the old rule of thumb to write five positive things about someone for every negative thought expressed.

What about those who are no longer part of your daily life because of a death, divorce, or another circumstance? Write about them as much as you are able or willing. This especially applies to those whose children or other relatives would benefit from knowing more about them.

You didn't live family life alone. Why would you want to record it alone? Enlist the help of your family for this chapter. Ask family members to fill out pages about themselves and their relationships with you, if possible. Having someone's description of herself and of her relationship with you is an important emotional artifact. You'll cherish those pages as a reminder of her and her interest in you. Where relationships have been less than healthy, consider writing the relationship pages yourself and expressing the way you wish things were.

Special Pages Suggestions

Special People

Special Places

Special Memories

Life-Changing

Experiences

Flashbulb Memories

Memorabilia

More

In Memoriam

On Your CD

My Pet

My Home

Adoption

Memories of My

Child's Adoption

The End of Our

Relationship

Solo Parenting

who have played significant roles in your adult years.
» If you had no children or romantic partner, you can remove those pages entirely.

» Missing information on a page shouldn't keep it out of your book. A single entry on a form makes it worth including.

About My Partner

Name

....
First   Middle   Surname (maiden/previous married)

....
Birth Date   (Day, Month, Year)

....
Birthplace

....
Death Date   Burial Location

> **TIP**
>
> Insert Memorabilia page with a copy of your partner's birth or infant baptismal certificate or other mementoes relating to information requested on this page.

Mother

Full Name ....

Race/ethnicity/nationality ....

Birth Date, Birthplace ....

Death Date, Place ....

Father

Full Name ....

Race/ethnicity/nationality ....

Birth Date, Birthplace..

Death Date, Place ....

Raised by (if not parents):

....
Names   Relation

Find additional copies of this page on your CD.

About My Partner

Where raised

....
Place(s) (and dates, if more than one place)

....
Place(s) (and dates, if more than one place)

Siblings

Name..
Birth Date, Birthplace...
Spouse...
Death Date, Place...

Name..
Birth Date, Birthplace...
Spouse...
Death Date, Place...

Name..
Birth Date, Birthplace...
Spouse...
Death Date, Place...

Religion

Family's religious denomination ....
Name of Congregation ....

Find additional copies of this page on your CD.

About My Partner

AS REMEMBERED BY _____

Education

....
High School   Place   Years Attended

....
College   Place   Years Attended

Health (significant illnesses, medical conditions, injuries)

....

....

....

....

Employment (including work in the home)

....

....

....

....

Hobbies (including volunteer activities, handicrafts, sports and
outdoor recreation, collections, etc.)

....

....

....

....

....

Find additional copies of this page on your CD.

About My Partner

Values and beliefs (including religious, civic, political, or other affiliations)

....

....

....

....

....

....

....

....

....

....

Additional Marriages/Romantic Partners (not including me)

Name of Spouse/Partner (include all former surnames)

....

Date of Ceremony and Place ....

If ended, date and how ....

Name of Spouse/Partner (include all former surnames)

....

Date of Ceremony and Place ....

If ended, date and how ....

Find additional copies of this page on your CD.

What was your partner like as a child? Describe his or her appearance and personality.

....

....

....

....

....

....

> **TIP**
>
> Have your partner fill this out about himself/herself, if possible. If you are filling out pages for more than one partner, write your partner's name across the top of the page.

Describe your partner's childhood community or neighborhood(s). Was it friendly or impersonal, crowded or isolated, urban or rural, safe or dangerous, rich or poor? Was everyone like your partner's family or did they stand out?

....

....

....

....

Describe your partner's home(s). Did he or she like where he or she lived? Describe any place in his or her home, yard, or neighborhood that was special to your partner. ....

....

....

....

....

Find additional copies of this page on your CD.

My Partner: Life Stories

_____

What were your partner's teenage years like? You might describe your partner's high-school experiences, what he or she did with free time (work or play), and important friendships.

....
....
....
....
....
....

Describe your partner's young-adult years: college, work, travel, romance, starting a family. What were your partner's favorite decisions and his or her regrets?

....
....
....
....
....
....

What are your goals for the future? You might mention hopes and dreams about your career/retirement, family, finances, personal enrichment, or leisure time.

....
....
....

Find additional copies of this page on your CD.

Our Dating Life

How did you two meet?

....

....

What attracted you to your partner?

....

....

What attracted your partner to you?

....

....

Describe your courtship or dating life. Mention special outings, funny moments, tender times.

....

....

When and how did you meet your partner's family? How did you feel? How did it go?

....

....

If you lived together while dating, when did you move in together? What led to your decision? Note memories about moving in together (or choosing not to).

....

....

....

Find additional copies of this page on your CD.

Our Engagement

How did you decide to get married? Describe the proposal.

....

....

....

If you formalized your engagement with a ring, write your memories about it.
(Describe the ring, picking it out, what made it special, etc.)

....

....

What was your engagement like? Long or short?
Did you spend a lot of time together? Live together or apart?

....

....

....

How did you feel during your engagement? Tell about moments of joy or doubt,
and any pressure from friends or family.

....

....

....

What prewedding celebrations did you have? Describe an engagement party,
bridal shower, bachelor/ette party, and/or rehearsal dinner.

....

....

....

Find additional copies of this page on your CD.

Our Wedding

....
Marriage Date   Place

....
Officiant   Title

Why we married there

....

....

Attendants   **Relationship to bride/groom**

....
Best Man

....
Matron/Maid of Honor

....
Bridesmaids

....
Bridesmaids

....
Groomsman

....
Groomsman

....
Ring Bearer

....
Flower Girl(s)

> **TIP**
>
> Insert Memorabilia
> pages with copies of
> wedding photos or
> marriage documents.
> If you fill out pages
> about more than one
> wedding, put your
> partner's name across
> the top of the page.

Find additional copies of this page on your CD.

Describe the wedding ceremony. Include details that are important to you
about the location or setting, clothing (dresses/tuxedos), the program, your rings,
the important participants, etc.

....

....

....

....

....

Describe the reception or other post-wedding celebration. Include details
that are important to you about the location, decorations, flowers, food, cake,
music, entertainment, etc.

....

....

....

....

Describe your honeymoon. Where did you go, and why, and for how long?
Recall tender or funny memories or mishaps.

....

....

....

....

Find additional copies of this page on your CD.

Think of your early time together, after your initial courtship/marriage. This might be your first year of marriage, the time period after moving in together, etc.

How did you spend time together as newlyweds (or as a newly committed couple)? Think of work, play, sports, hobbies, dates, or just hanging out.

....

....

....

....

How did you feel when you were together? Apart?

....

....

....

Write about a happy event or moment with your partner during this time.

....

....

....

....

What struggles did you have in your relationship? How did you handle them?

....

....

....

Find additional copies of this page on your CD.

Newlyweds

_____

What were your circumstances like at this time (financial, health, family issues, etc)? How did you handle them?

....

....

....

Write about an experience that made you grow closer as a couple.

....

....

....

Write about an experience that pulled you apart as a couple. How did you handle it?

....

....

....

What important lessons did you learn (yourself or as a couple) during this time?

....

....

....

How did each of you change, adapt, or sacrifice during this time for the sake of your relationship? How do you wish you or your partner had changed?

....

....

....

Find additional copies of this page on your CD.

Building a Life Together

_____

Think of your time together after you settled in as a couple. This might be the time following your first year as a couple, or after you became parents, etc. (Parenting as a couple is addressed in another section.) If you fill out this form for more than one partner, write your partner's name across the top of the page.

When you got over the newness or novelty of being together, how did your feelings about your partner change or grow?

....

....

....

After you'd been together for a while, how did you spend your free time together? How important to you was spending time together?

....

....

....

Write about a happy time with your partner during this time.

....

....

....

What struggles did you have in your relationship? How did you handle them?

....

....

....

Find additional copies of this page on your CD.

Building a Life Together

What were your circumstances like at this time (financial, health, family issues, etc)? How did you handle them?

....

....

....

Write about an experience that made you grow closer as a couple.

....

....

....

Write about an experience that pulled you apart as a couple. How did you handle it?

....

....

....

What important lessons did you learn (yourself or as a couple) during this time?

....

....

....

How did each of you change, adapt, or sacrifice during this time for the sake of your relationship? How do you wish you or your partner had changed?

....

....

....

....

Find additional copies of this page on your CD.

My Partner Today

What do you love most about your partner right now?

....

....

....

....

....

> **TIP**
>
> Fill out this form if you have a living partner; have your partner fill out a copy about you, too.

What about your partner is challenging or difficult for you?

....

....

....

....

When it's just the two of you at home, what is your partner like?

....

....

....

....

What is your partner like in a public or social setting? What kinds of public or social settings does your partner enjoy (or avoid)?

....

....

....

Find additional copies of this page on your CD.

My Partner Today

Describe your partner's sense of humor. Give an example of something your partner would find funny or entertaining.

....

....

....

What kinds of challenges does your partner handle well? What kinds of situations are difficult for your partner?

....

....

....

How would you describe your partner's values or beliefs today? How have those beliefs grown or changed in your time together?

....

....

....

What is an admirable quality or skill your partner has that you lack?

....

....

....

What do you miss about your partner when you're not together?

....

....

....

Find additional copies of this page on your CD.

Parenting With My Partner

How did you feel when you learned you would
be a parent? How did your partner feel?

....

....

Write about your experience as a couple during
pregnancy or adoption. How did you handle your
stresses and/or excitement?

....

....

....

> **TIP**
>
> Fill out this page for
> any partner with
> whom you had a
> natural/adopted child
> (your partner could
> fill it out, too). If you
> were a solo parent, fill
> out the Solo Parenting
> form instead of (or in
> addition to) this one.

Describe a special or tender moment you shared as
expectant or new parents.

....

....

What changed about your relationship when you became parents?
How did you handle the changes?

....

....

How did your daily lives (work, leisure, etc.) change when you had children?
How did you and your partner handle these changes?

....

....

....

Find additional copies of this page on your CD.

Parenting With My Partner

What did you do well as a new parent? What did your partner do well?
What did you or your partner struggle with as new parents?

....

....

What parenting responsibilities did you share when your child(ren) was an
infant? What about later? How did you feel about your division of parenting
responsibilities?

....

....

Describe your parenting style compared to your partner's. How did these
similarities or differences affect your relationship? Your child(ren)?

....

....

What changes or growth in yourself have you seen as a result of being a parent?

....

....

Who has been a source of support to you as parents? What kind of support
have they offered? What difference has it made in your lives?

....

....

....

....

....

Find additional copies of this page on your CD.

About My Child

....

First   Middle   Last Name

....

Birth Date (Day, Month, Year)

Place of Birth

....

Hospital (or other location)

....

Address

....

Delivered by

....

Other parent's name

TIP

Fill one out for each child. (If your child was adopted, fill out two additional forms from your CD, Adoption and Memories of My Child's Adoption.)

Describe your memories of your child's birth. If you were not present, write what you know about your child's birth.

....

....

....

....

....

....

....

....

Find additional copies of this page on your CD.

About My Child

My Child's Education

....
School Name   Place   Years Attended

....
School Name   Place   Years Attended

....
School Name   Place   Years Attended

....
School Name   Place   Years Attended

Religion

Share memories of these events on Special Memories pages. Put copies of certificates, photos, etc. on Memorabilia pages.

Religious Affiliation(s):

....
Rite   Date   Place   Officiant

....
Witnesses, godparents, or other special participants

....
Rite   Date   Place   Officiant

....
Witnesses, godparents, or other special participants

....
Rite   Date   Place   Officiant

....
Witnesses, godparents, or other special participants

Find additional copies of this page on your CD.

Memories of My Child

What did your child look like as a baby and/or young child? Mention any family resemblances.

· ·

· ·

· ·

> **TIP**
>
> Insert Memorabilia pages with copies of photos of your child at various ages, including photos with you and/or the child's other parent.

What was your child's personality like as a baby or toddler? You might describe mannerisms, social skills, and likes or dislikes.

· ·

· ·

· ·

What did you enjoy most about your child when he or she was young?

· ·

· ·

· ·

· ·

What was your child's health like as a baby or child (wellness, illnesses, injuries)?

· ·

· ·

· ·

· ·

Find additional copies of this page on your CD.

Memories of My Child

AS REMEMBERED BY _____

As your child grew, did he or she remind you of yourself or another loved one?
In what ways? ....
....
....

How did your growing child show his or her independence?
....
....
....

What did you admire most about your child during his/her teenage or
young adult years? ....
....
....

Write about choices your teen or young adult made that were difficult for you.
Why were they difficult? How did they turn out?
....
....
....

Describe anything you wish you'd done differently while raising your child.
....
....
....
....

Find additional copies of this page on your CD.

Everyday Life With My Children

AS REMEMBERED BY _____

When your children were young, what was your daily routine like?

....

....

....

When your children reached school age, what was the after-school routine like?

....

....

....

What did your family do on weekends or other days off?

....

....

....

What did your family do during the summers? (Document travel on a
Travel Log or Special Memories form.)

....

....

What kinds of foods did your family eat? Describe mealtimes and favorite foods.
Did one member of the family prepare special meals or desserts?

....

....

Find additional copies of this page on your CD.

Everyday Life With My Children

AS REMEMBERED BY _____

Was your home clean, cluttered, or chaotic? Who took charge of neatness?

....

....

What chores did your children do? How did you motivate them to do their

chores? ....

....

What television shows, radio programs, or books did your family enjoy?

....

....

Did you take your children to the movies or the theater? Share memories of a

favorite show or a fun time out.

....

....

Describe your family pets. Who took care of them? (Use the My Pet form on your

CD to honor pets you really loved.)

....

....

How did your professional life (and/or that of your partner) affect your family life?

Would you do things differently if you could?

....

....

....

Find additional copies of this page on your CD.

My Grown-Up Child

Describe the path your child's life has taken since youth (education, work, family life, etc.).

....

....

....

> **TIP**
>
> If possible, have your children fill out this form about themselves. If one of your children lived to adulthood but is no longer living, fill out as much information as is appropriate.

Describe his or her health during these years (well-being, illnesses, injuries).

....

....

....

What have been some of his or her challenges during these years?

....

....

....

What have been some of his or her successes during these years?

....

....

....

What have been his or her most rewarding relationships during these years? The most difficult relationships?

....

....

....

Find additional copies of this page on your CD.

My Grown-Up Child

What are your child's favorite pastimes?

....

....

What are your child's goals or hopes for the future? (If he or she is not living, what were his or her goals or hopes in the last years of life, and were they realized?)

....

....

Marriages

Name (include all former surnames) ....

Date of Ceremony and Place ....

If ended, date and how ....

Name (include all former surnames) ....

Date of Ceremony and Place ....

If ended, date and how ....

Children

....

| Name | Gender | Birth Date | Birthplace |

....

| Name | Gender | Birth Date | Birthplace |

....

| Name | Gender | Birth Date | Birthplace |

....

| Name | Gender | Birth Date | Birthplace |

Find additional copies of this page on your CD.

About My Grandchild

Fill out this form for each grandchild and insert it behind his or her parent's form.

Full Name . . . .

Birth Date and Place . . . .

Mother's full name (include maiden name) . . . .

Father's full name . . . .

Family's religious affiliation, if any . . . .

Name of Congregation . . . .

Marriages

Name (include all former surnames) . . . .

Date of Ceremony and Place . . . .

If ended, date and how . . . .

Name (include all former surnames) . . . .

Date of Ceremony and Place . . . .

If ended, date and how . . . .

Children

Name	Gender	Birth Date	Birthplace
Name	Gender	Birth Date	Birthplace
Name	Gender	Birth Date	Birthplace
Name	Gender	Birth Date	Birthplace

Find additional copies of this page on your CD.

About My Grandchild

AS REMEMBERED BY _____

Write your memories and feelings about your grandchild's birth or adoption.

....

....

How would you describe your grandchild's personality and appearance? Does he or she remind you of other family members?

....

....

What has your relationship with this grandchild been like throughout his or her life? How do you feel about your relationship?

....

....

Write about any milestones in your grandchild's life (religious, cultural, educational, etc).

....

....

What interests does your grandchild have? How are they reflected in his or her life?

....

....

What do you love most about your grandchild?

....

What advice would you give your grandchild for now or the future?

....

Find additional copies of this page on your CD.

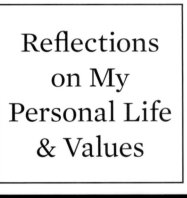

8

Reflections on My Personal Life & Values

This chapter celebrates the person you are today, from your daily routines to your friendships. It helps you describe the unique space you have carved for yourself in this world. Topics include:

» **Daily Life.** The routines, rituals, places, and pastimes of your everyday life.

» **My Home.** Your current abode, be it dorm, apartment, condo, house, etc, along with its quirks and qualities.

» **My Pet.** Any furry, four-legged, or otherwise nonhuman, friends you have.

» **Friendships.** Who your best buddies are, what you do together, and your own role as a friend.

» **My Hobbies.** Whatever you like to create or do for fun.

» **My Heritage.** Your sense of your family legacy, your own personal traditions, and their meaning to you.

» **My Values and Beliefs.** The standards, rules, or beliefs you live by, and why you live by them.

» **My Hopes and Dreams.** What you want to accomplish or be, and what you wish you could be.

» **My Legacy.** The memories you want to share with future generations.

Memorabilia

Insert a current photo of yourself.

What do you like about your appearance now?

....

....

....

What, if anything, do you wish were a little different?

....

....

....

Daily Life

What's an average day like for you? What about your "days off"?

....
....
....
....

What do you wear most days? What's your favorite outfit or piece of clothing?

....
....
....
....

What are some of your habits or routines (e.g, morning coffee and paper, Sunday brunch, daily walks, can't miss TV show, mass every morning, Facebook every five minutes)?

....
....
....
....

What do you do to unwind or relax?

....
....
....

Find additional copies of this page on your CD.

Daily Life

What modern technologies or gadgets do you rely on in everyday life?

....

....

....

....

Where do you go to eat out, or for drinks or dessert? How often do you go? Any restaurants you love for special occasions?

....

....

....

....

How do you get where you're going—walk, ride, or drive? If you have a car, what's it like, and what do you think of it?

....

....

....

....

When you have extra money to spend, what (and who) do you spend it on?

....

....

....

Find additional copies of this page on your CD.

My Home

Address

....

Monthly rent or mortgage amount ....

Suggestion: If current, you may want to withhold this
for security or privacy reasons.

Move-in date: ....

Who lives with me:

....

....

....

....

Describe your home (size, style, condition, layout).

....

....

....

....

What's your favorite spot in your home? Why do you love it?

....

....

....

....

Add details about previous homes on additional copies of this page on your CD.

TIP

Use a Special Places page to remember other places in which you've spent a lot of time, like a family cabin, cottage, condo, or annual vacation destination.

My Home

Describe your neighborhood.

....

....

....

....

How have you made the space your own (remodeling, decorating, landscaping, gardening, furniture, etc.)?

....

....

....

....

What do you enjoy about your home?

....

....

....

....

What don't you like about your home?

....

....

....

....

Find additional copies of this page on your CD.

My Pet

Use a page for each pet; place them here or in the appropriate section of your life (childhood, etc).

TIP

Place photos of your pet on a Memorabilia page.

....
Name

....
Birth Date or Approximate Age

....
Adoption Date

....
Breed   Gender

How did you get your pet?

....

Describe your pet's physical appearance and personality.

....

....

How do you feel about your pet?

....

....

Who takes care of your pet?

....

....

What games or activities do you and your pet do together?

....

Find additional copies of this page on your CD.

My Pet

What are your pet's favorites (treats, toys, places, pastimes, people)? Least favorites?

....

....

....

....

Where does your pet sleep? (Is this where you want your pet to sleep?)

....

....

....

....

What adventures have you and your pet enjoyed together (travel, hikes, play dates, pet charity events)?

....

....

....

....

Describe celebrations that include your pet (birthdays, holidays, annual photo portraits). ....

....

....

....

Find additional copies of this page on your CD.

Friendships

Who would you say are your closest friends now? Why are you such good friends? What do you do together?...

....

....

....

....

Describe your larger circle of friends or acquaintances. Where do you see them? How often? What do you enjoy about these friends (or groups of friends)?

....

....

....

....

TIP

Include friends' pictures or correspondence on Memorabilia pages. Consider including a Special People page for each of your closest friends, past and present. Consider placing pages with past friends in the appropriate section (teen years, etc).

Write about a friendship that is no longer part of your life that you miss. Who was this friend, and why was that person special to you? What happened, and how do you feel about it?

....

....

....

....

....

Find additional copies of this page on your CD.

Friendships

What kind of friend are you? What do you think your friends enjoy about you?
What are your weaknesses as a friend?

....

....

....

....

Describe memories of special occasions you have celebrate with friends.

....

....

....

....

Write about a time a friend helped you in an important way.
What did it mean to you?...

....

....

....

Write about a time you helped out a friend, and what it meant to you
(and/or that friend). ....

....

....

....

Find additional copies of this page on your CD.

My Hobbies

What activities have you enjoyed in your spare time throughout your life?

....

....

....

....

What activities do you currently enjoy? How much time do you spend on them?

....

....

....

....

What kinds of hobby equipment, tools, supplies, magazines/books, etc., do you own? Which have you used the most?

....

....

....

....

Describe something you have built or otherwise created. Are you proud of it?

....

....

....

....

Find additional copies of this page on your CD.

My Interests

If someone hands you a newspaper, which section will you read first? Which won't you read at all? Why? What kind of magazines do you enjoy?

....

....

What kinds of television shows and/or movies do you enjoy?

....

....

What kinds of events or attractions do you like to attend (exhibits, museums, fairs, charity events, community dinners, races, festivals, concerts, etc.)?

....

....

What kind of music do you enjoy now? Favorite radio station? Band? Album?

....

....

What do you like to read? How much time do you spend reading?

....

....

What do you do for sports, outdoor recreation, or exercise (if you do these)?

....

....

What kinds of things do you not enjoy?

....

....

Find additional copies of this page on your CD.

My Heritage

What values or principles did your parents, grandparents, or other relatives instill in you? In other words, what does your family name mean to you?

....

....

....

....

....

....

....

....

....

Describe family traditions you have continued to celebrate as an adult.
Who participates? What do these traditions mean to you?

....

....

....

....

....

....

....

....

....

My Heritage

Describe traditions you have created yourself (or with a family of your own) as an adult. Who participates? What do these traditions mean to you?

....

....

....

....

....

As an adult, how have you observed birthdays with your loved ones?

....

....

....

....

....

....

As an adult, what food traditions have you created or passed on? Are there special foods or recipes among your loved ones now? Does one person in your circle of love do the cooking or baking? ....

....

....

....

....

....

My Values and Beliefs

Describe your religious and/or philosophical beliefs. How have these changed over time?..

....

....

....

Describe your political, social, and/or cultural views. How have these changed over time?..

....

....

....

Who are your heroes? Why?..

....

....

....

What is a cause or political/moral issue you have passionately supported? Why?

....

....

....

What is a political/moral issue or cause you have passionately opposed? Why?

....

....

My Values and Beliefs

What is a political/moral issue or cause that you feel conflicted or unsure about, or that you have changed your position on? Why?

....

....

....

What would you say are the values that guide your life?

....

....

....

Have your beliefs been dramatically influenced by one event, book, etc.? What was it? How did it change you?

....

....

....

What causes, if any, do you support now (humanitarian, religious, environmental, political, social, animal rights, etc.)? How do you show your support?

....

....

....

What do you consider a personality or character flaw about yourself that you wish you could change? Why?

....

....

....

My Hopes and Dreams

What is a goal you are actively working on now? Why do you want to achieve it? How confident are you of success? ....

....

....

....

What is a goal you would like to accomplish but haven't yet?

....

....

....

....

What is a goal you wish you could accomplish but probably never will?

....

....

....

....

What hopes and dreams do you have for your future?

....

....

....

....

....

My Hopes and Dreams

What would you do with all your time now if you were suddenly freed from your current obligations? ....

....

....

....

....

....

....

....

If you could choose your career or life's work all over again, what would you do? Why? ....

....

....

....

....

....

....

....

If you could visit or live anywhere in the world for a time, where it would be, and why? ....

....

....

Date

My Legacy

What do you hope people will remember about you?

My Legacy

What advice do you have for future generations?

....

....

....

....

....

....

....

....

....

....

....

....

....

....

....

....

....

....

....

....

....

....

....

9

Preserving Your Memories

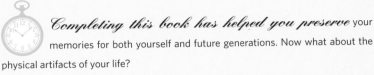 *Completing this book has helped you preserve* your memories for both yourself and future generations. Now what about the physical artifacts of your life?

The "stuff of life" is also precious and worth preserving. Your treasures might be shoeboxes full of photos and memorabilia. Or it might be a vintage wedding gown, jewelry, or artwork. Most households have important papers that deserve preservation, too: recipes, letters, birth certificates, news clippings about family members, etc. How can you organize, identify, preserve, and share these?

What to Keep

The first question to ask yourself is, "What do I have?" People can be surprised by what's lurking in bottom drawers, attics, and basements. Take a thorough tour of your home's nooks and crannies. Look for anything you've kept for sentimental or historical value. Your grandparents' marriage certificate and your mother's hope chest are obvious examples. But also look for items that will *become* heirlooms if you care for them properly, like your favorite childhood book or the birth announcement samplers your mother-in-law cross-stitched for each of your children. Don't overlook heirlooms hiding in plain sight: the quilt on your guest bed that Grandma made, or your great-grandmother's butterfly pin in the back of your jewelry box. Make a quick mental or physical inventory of your findings.

Next, consider carefully what's worth keeping indefinitely. You may be thinking *What?!? Shouldn't I keep every item of sentimental value?* The answer is no. As you read through this chapter and learn more about properly preserving your treasures, you'll find that many require pricey archival containers and/or particular storage conditions. When you see the preservation cost, you may be less willing to keep four hundred photos of your mother's cats. Or you may quickly realize that the only truly heirloom-friendly storage space in your home is a shelf or two in a shallow closet.

So how do you identify which family treasures are most precious to you? Well, if you were moving across the world tomorrow and could only take one sentimental object, what it would be? A close relative's personal belongings are often at the top of the list, imbued as they are with emotional memories.

Which heirlooms are not as important to your legacy? These would be the items with no personal connection to yourself, like the wireless radio set you rescued from your neighbor's estate sale or large numbers of mass-produced trinkets. Also consider items that won't be as meaningful to future generations, like three rolls of panoramic photos of the Grand Canyon with nary a relative in sight.

Here are some suggestions for your surplus heirlooms:

1. Keep one small part of a large group, like a single place setting of china or one section of a deteriorated quilt, and display it.

2. Photograph or scan items before finding them a new home.

3. Document artifacts that shed light on a person's life before disposing of them. As you're culling your father's bookshelf, record the names of all the books before you sell or donate them. Describe a collection or group of photos, and how their existence reminds you of a special person's character. (Documenting artifacts is covered in more detail later in this chapter.)

4. Share the items with others who will treasure the legacy. This doesn't mean you should dump unwanted junk at your brother's house. But you could create a photo album for your brother from your duplicate photos or let him look through collections and pick out a few favorites to keep.

5. Sell a large-ticket item you don't need and use the proceeds to invest in your heritage. For example, sell Mom's fur coat at a consignment shop, then purchase a preservation kit for her wedding dress.

6. Donate an item to a cause your relative loved: Send your father's limited edition wildlife art print to the local humane society fundraiser.

7. Still can't part with it? Find a reason to keep it. Give it new life in your living space. Hang a textile, document, or other flat artifact on the wall. Start using Grandma's china. Give Dad's stamp collection to your son and help him add to it.

Document Your Heirlooms

After divesting yourself of extra stuff, you're ready to document the true treasures you've kept. You can do it quickly with a free Heirloom Inventory Form like that found at *Family Tree Magazine*'s website <www.familytreemagazine.com/FreeForms>. A more thorough approach (which will be especially appreciated by loved ones when settling your estate) is to take pictures of your heirlooms and caption them with descriptions in photo albums, on scrapbook pages, or in the Family Heirlooms and Family Recipes sections of *Family Tree Legacies: Preserving Memories Throughout Time* by Allison Stacy and Diane Haddad.

Remember, an unidentified heirloom will someday become just another garage sale trinket. It's the people and memories that make an object an heirloom.

What should you identify about an heirloom?

Provenance: Who and where it came from. Who made or purchased it originally? Why did they have it? Who else has owned it? How did it come to you? Give detailed explanations; include relatives' full names, where they lived, and other explanatory notes, like a profession or interest that led to them create or own the object.

Documentation: You can more fully establish provenance by documenting your heirloom. Original receipts, the owner's manual, a letter mentioning the item, a photograph of the owner wearing it, etc.: All offer further evidence of the importance and authenticity of this heirloom to your personal or family story. If you have had an item professionally restored, repaired, etc., include reports from those who did the work.

Stories and memories: Why is this heirloom valuable to you? Explain your sentimental attachment to the object. Write your memories and, as previously mentioned, place them in an album or binder along with photographs of the heirloom.

Appraisal or other statement of financial value: Some items, by nature of their age and originality, have financial as well as sentimental value. If you have had an item appraised, include the appraiser's report. If an item has been insured, include the proper paperwork.

Preserve

As you take a closer look at your heirlooms, you may notice some in less-than-perfect condition. Of course, everything ages. Even items that look brand-new will gradually deteriorate. How they change depends both on the artifacts themselves (what they're made of) and how they're stored. Fortunately, you can slow down or minimize damage to your personal and family treasures. The answer may be as simple as unfolding a blanket or moving a photograph out of direct sunlight. Other techniques require a little more investment of time, money, and research.

For items that are significantly damaged or appear to be actively deteriorating, consider consulting a conservator. Find one through groups such as the American Institute for Conservation of Historic and Artistic Works <www.conservation-us.org>. A conservator can use proven, minimally invasive methods to repair or restore an heirloom and advise you on proper storage materials and conditions for a particular type of material (silk, parchment, ivory, wood, etc.) or construction (embroidery, scrapbooks, furniture, etc.).

Take a close look at your heirlooms. Do they show breakage, crumbling, tearing, staining, fading, permanent crease marks, water or pest damage, etc.? Generally, if your document or other object is in good condition and doesn't seem to be actively deteriorating, you can preserve it as is by packing and storing it properly.

Packing

When it comes to packaging heirlooms for storage, use archival supplies purchased from a reputable vendor. These are pricier than your average manila file folder or cardboard box because they have extra manufacturing costs to remove acids and lignin. Acids are used in the paper-making process to break up wood fibers. Residues of those acids remain in ordinary paper and cardboard, and this residue makes paper deteriorate over time. *Lignin* is a natural plant polymer that's good for the living plant but causes slow chemical damage once the plant is made into paper. Archival-grade paper products have had most of the acid and lignin removed during manufacturing (watch for the terms acid-free and lignin-free on paper products, including boxes).

Buffered paper and boxes contain an alkaline buffering agent that provides further safeguards against acids that remain in the paper. Archival boxes also are constructed with special adhesives that won't damage paper over time.

Some inert plastics are used in archival storage products, namely polyester (often known by popular brand names Mylar D or Melinex), polyethylene, and polypropylene. You'll find this material in plastic sleeves used to protect documents and photos. Polyvinyl acetate (PVA) is often used in conservation when adhesive is required. Be careful when choosing off-brand plastic products or those that don't specifically name the type of plastic used. A common plastic, polyvinyl chloride (PVC), emits damaging gases (ever smelled a new plastic shower curtain?) and is not safe for your heirloom storage.

Though some plastics can be used safely, avoid suffocating artifacts by sealing them entirely in air-tight plastic containers. While this might seem a great solution for safely storing items in a damp basement, you'll also trap damaging moisture, gases, etc., *inside* the container.

Specific artifacts will respond best to specific storage products and methods. For example, buffered tissue, papers, and boxes should be used only with heirlooms made from plant-based materials (papers, undyed cotton, linen, etc.). Store paper and fabric items unfolded, or with as few folds as possible (refold them in a different direction every so often to prevent permanent creasing), with archival tissue cushioning the folds and hollows.

Try to preserve original order and grouping of documents and photos, as their positioning near each other may tell a story. Within the original order, separate different types of materials (news clippings, photos, etc.) from each other in archival sleeves to prevent acid and ink migration and other damage.

Learn more about archival techniques for specific materials in *Saving Stuff: How to Care for and Preserve Your Collectibles, Heirlooms, and Other Prized Possessions* by Don Williams and Louisa Jagger; *Organizing and Preserving Your Heirloom Documents* by Katherine Scott Sturdevant, and the *Guide to Collections Care: Paper, Photographs, Textiles & Books*, a free brochure available from Gaylord <www.gaylord.com>. Find a crib sheet for care of common heirlooms in the Family Heirlooms section of *Family Tree Legacies: Preserving Memories throughout Time* by Allison Stacy and Diane Haddad. Online, look to websites of reputed archiving sources such as The National Institute for Conservation <www.heritagepreservation.org>, The Smithsonian Museum Conservation Institute <si.edu/mci>, and various state or university archives. The Practical Archivist website <http://practicalarchivist.com>, hosted by professional archivist Sally Jacobs, also provides readable and fun insights on storing your family stuff.

A final word about choosing products: The term "archival" is not regulated. Neither are product descriptions like "great for photo storage." Choose products from vendors who have built their reputations on providing trustworthy supplies for archives, museums, and home archivists like you. See a partial list of these at the end of this chapter.

It won't do you any good to pamper your heirlooms in archival packaging if they are hidden away in musty basements, hot attics, or unregulated storage units. The rule of thumb is to store your treasures in the same conditions in which people like to live: moderate temperatures and low humidity. (Yes, this limits how much you can keep, unless your home has abundant closets or square footage.) Additionally, think about water pipes or other potentially harmful household objects near your heirlooms, even behind walls. Consider whether pests might be a problem; you don't want mice nesting in your wedding tux or bugs eating the bookbinding glue from your grandfather's diary. If you are going to display your items, keep them out of direct or strong light, and out of the reach of sticky fingers or curious cat paws.

Share

We may safeguard heirlooms for our own enjoyment, but most of us have an eye to the future. We eventually want to share our stuff with loved ones. Passing on heirlooms can strengthen trust and understanding between family members. It perpetuates your legacy and can instill a sense of heritage in both young and old.

Lots of questions can surface when you start planning to share your heirlooms. Who should receive them? How do you divide a limited number of treasures among many relatives? Should you separate collections? What if you're not sure your mementoes will be sufficiently cared for or appreciated?

One way you can share family artifacts without having to part with them permanently is to put them on display in your home. When others visit, you can tell the stories behind them. There are some risks; artifacts might be damaged by exposure to everyday life. But you might deem that a small price to pay for the ability to enjoy and share your legacy any time while keeping it safe at home. Here are some suggestions for display:

1. Frame an antique photo, a small heirloom textile, or a copy of a family document or letter. Consult a professional framer for tips on framing these items without harming them. Hang these in areas that don't receive direct light, like hallways.

2. Arrange small mementoes or collections in a shadowbox frame, which is a deep frame that accommodates dimensional objects. Group objects to tell a story, like a rosary, missal, holy card, and photo of a First Communion, or a collection of trinkets from Grandpa's desk. A professional framer can help you mount some objects safely for vertical display (do not permanently adhere them to any surfaces). Otherwise, display your frame horizontally. Include a variety of sizes and materials for greater interest, and your handwritten or typed caption.

3. Include a conversation-starting artifact as part of your home's décor. Stack Grandpa's favorite books on a shelf with his spectacles perched on top; spread handstitched linen napkins on a sideboard or a homespun quilt on a guest bed. Display linens only in little-used areas where damage is unlikely; try to display them unfolded.

4. Create an album of heirloom photos with detailed captions. Keep it out, like a coffee-table book, with every expectation of it being thumbed through. Be sure your album is made of archival materials and ensure that your photos are protected under clear archival pages.

When you are ready to part with heirlooms, consider both the artifact and the potential recipient. Chances are much better that your gift will be appreciated and well-cared for if given to someone who has shown interest in your family history, though certainly you can give heritage gifts in an effort to *awaken* interest. It's ideal if you can match a relative with an artifact he or she would love: an old tool, book, vintage jewelry, etc. Finally, consider whether the person has space, savvy, and likely willingness to care for an heirloom. If the person moves frequently or doesn't tend to keep items of sentimental value, you might first inquire before gifting a precious object.

Don't overlook the value of small, simple heirlooms—or what they might mean to a relative you don't know well. Your gifts don't need to be grand gestures. The littlest mementoes—a smooth glass bead, a watch fob, a business card—can become treasures simply for having belonged to an ancestor.

Once you've determined to give an heirloom gift, consider taking a few extra steps to ensure the gift can be appreciated for a long time. Many of the displays mentioned earlier make great gifts: anything in a frame, shadowbox, or another container. If you are giving a textile or another fragile object, present it already wrapped in archival packaging. (Explain the packaging so the recipient doesn't throw away the tissues or boxes!) Don't forget that every heirloom gift should come with a written explanation of the object's provenance and significance to yourself and/or your family.

Old photos and documents are easy and inexpensive to copy and frame for more than one relative. Consider creating similar gifts—framed color copies of Grandma's watercolor paintings or a handsome display of family photos—for everyone at the holidays, especially when a family is large. When creating a photo display (particularly from different eras), consider printing all the images in black and white or sepia tone (browns) for a uniform, attractive look. Many basic photo editing software packages will do this for your digital images; be sure to preserve a digital image with its original coloring, too.

If you have old family papers that aren't easy to copy, like a diary or faded letters, consider transcribing them into typed form. Create a binder or book for loved ones to enjoy. Add a description of those who penned the documents and a photo of the authors if you have one.

Do you have some creative skills? Consider making over less-usable family artifacts into something new. A broken piece of furniture might be retooled into a walking stick or a simple paperweight that shows the wood grain at its best. Your father's old ties or your mother's favorite floral shirts could be refashioned into a quilt or pillow (it might surprise you how well people recognize fabrics worn by their loved ones). Again, consider the objects and those who will receive them: What kind of gift would they appreciate?

Some family archivists wonder whether they should try to keep an heirloom collection intact or parcel it out among many relatives. The collection might be a full set of monogrammed china, folk art collected during a loved one's travels, or a more traditional stamp or coin collection. Consider whether the original owner would have wanted a painstakingly gathered collection of historic or cultural artifacts to remain together. If so, perhaps the most fitting legacy would be to donate the collection to an appropriate repository in the family member's name, and keep images of the items. If you care more about sharing these among your family members, document the collection as a whole before distributing it, and keep a record of what was distributed to whom.

Document collections often have the most historical and genealogical value when they remain together. Parceling out the ten love letters your grandparents wrote each other might please ten great-grandchildren, but their ability to tell your grandparents' stories lessens when the items are separated. Again, consider sharing copies, but try to keep original documents together.

Finally, think about your wishes for the heirlooms that remain in your possession during your lifetime. Mention important ones specifically in your will; indicate where they are in your home and who should receive them. Be sure the stories of these artifacts get passed along, either through letters included with your estate documents or in an heirloom inventory like the kinds previously mentioned (give your executor a copy of the heirloom log, or mention its location in your will). Not only will your heirlooms end up with the right people, your grieving relatives won't have the difficult and often tense experience of trying to divide family mementoes amongst themselves. Even when heirlooms are not specifically mentioned in your will, an accessible heirloom inventory may prevent your grandfather's quilt from being donated to the local thrift store.

It does take time, energy and sometimes money to properly document, maintain, and distribute family heirlooms. But these artifacts were likely not accumulated in a day, and you don't need to have them all neatly wrapped up in a day, either. Just as you took the time to savor your memories as you told your stories in this book, take whatever time you can to savor—and save—the memories behind your meaningful possessions. Share them in any number of ways, but do share them somehow, so they can be heirlooms in someone else's life someday, continuing the task of reminding that person of his or her legacy just as the items have for you.

Archival Products Vendors

» Archival Products
www.archival.com
800-526-5640

» Gaylord
www.gaylord.com
800-962-9580

» Hollinger Metal Edge
www.hollingermetaledge.com
800-634-0491

» Talas
www.talasonline.com
212-219-0770

» University Products
www.universityproducts.com
800-628-1912

10

Special Forms

Special People

Name ....

Relationship ....

About this person and our relationship:...

....

....

....

....

....

....

....

....

Continue on a More page as needed.

What this person has meant to me:...

....

....

....

....

....

....

....

....

Continue on a More page as needed. Find additional copies of this page on your CD.

Special People

Name ....

Relationship ....

About this person and our relationship:..
....
....
....
....
....
....
....
....

Continue on a More page as needed.

What this person has meant to me:..
....
....
....
....
....
....
....
....

Continue on a More page as needed. Find additional copies of this page on your CD.

Special Places

Honor a particular place that has been meaningful to you, whether it was an entire city or your grandparents' back porch.

Name of Place ....

Location ....

Write a description of this place.

....

....

....

....

....

....

....

Why was this place was special to you?

....

....

....

....

....

....

....

....

Find additional copies of this page on your CD.

Special Places

_____

Honor a particular place that has been meaningful to you, whether it was an entire city or your grandparents' back porch.

Name of Place ....

Location ....

Write a description of this place.

....

....

....

....

....

....

....

Why was this place was special to you?

....

....

....

....

....

....

....

....

Find additional copies of this page on your CD.

Special Memories

Event ....

Date/Time Period ....

Location ....

Write your memory. Tell who was involved and describe what you were doing.
Use full names and specific details.

....

....

....

....

....

....

....

Why is this memory so special to you?

....

....

....

....

....

....

....

Find additional copies of this page on your CD.

Special Memories

_____

Event ....

Date/Time Period ....

Location ....

Write your memory. Tell who was involved and describe what you were doing.
Use full names and specific details.

....

....

....

....

....

....

....

Why is this memory so special to you?

....

....

....

....

....

....

....

Find additional copies of this page on your CD.

Life-Changing Experience

Event ....

Date/Time Period ....

Location ....

Write your memories of this experience. Who was involved and what happened?
Use specific details.

....

....

....

....

....

....

....

How did this experience change the way you thought or felt or lived your life? Use
specific details: what you thought or felt, or the differences you noticed in yourself.

....

....

....

....

....

....

Find additional copies of this page on your CD.

Flashbulb Memories

Your vivid recollection of a highly public event, like a natural or man-made disaster or the assassination of a public figure.

....

Where were you when you heard about this public event?

....

....

....

How did you hear about it?

....

....

....

How did you react? How did others around you react?

....

....

....

What images, sounds, or other details do you remember about that day?

....

....

....

Did your life change (or a loved one's life) in consequence of this important event?

....

....

Find additional copies of this page on your CD.

Memorabilia

Adhere copies of important documents, photos, postcards, or other memorabilia to this page. Insert this page in the appropriate section of your book. Do not adhere original documents, photographs, or other valuable one-of-a-kind materials to this page. Those should be stored in an archival environment.

Describe the item featured on this page, its significance, and the location of the original if the item is a copy.

....

....

....

....

Find additional copies of this page on your CD.

Memorabilia

Adhere copies of important documents, photos, postcards, or other memorabilia to this page. Insert this page in the appropriate section of your book. Do not adhere original documents, photographs, or other valuable one-of-a-kind materials to this page. Those should be stored in an archival environment.

Describe the item featured on this page, its significance, and the location of the original if the item is a copy.

....

....

....

....

Find additional copies of this page on your CD.

More

Page continued from..
Section/Page Header

....
....
....
....
....
....
....
....
....
....
....
....
....
....
....
....
....
....
....

Find additional copies of this page on your CD.

More

Page continued from...
Section/Page Header

....

....

....

....

....

....

....

....

....

....

....

....

....

....

....

....

....

Find additional copies of this page on your CD.

On a Memorabilia page, attach a copy of a funeral card, obituary, photo of a tombstone, or another memento relating to this person's passing.

In memory of ....

Relationship to you ....

Date and place of death ....

Circumstances and/or cause of death ....

Location of funeral ....

Location of burial ....

Describe the last memorable time you spent with this person.

....

....

....

Write some thoughts or feelings about this person, or about losing this person.

....

....

....

....

What do you wish you could tell or ask this person?

....

....

....

Find additional copies of this page on your CD.

In Memoriam

AS REMEMBERED BY _____

On a Memorabilia page, attach a copy of a funeral card, obituary, photo of a tombstone, or another memento relating to this person's passing.

In memory of ....

Relationship to you ....

Date and place of death ....

Circumstances and/or cause of death ....

Location of funeral ....

Location of burial ....

Describe the last memorable time you spent with this person.

....

....

....

Write some thoughts or feelings about this person, or about losing this person.

....

....

....

....

What do you wish you could tell or ask this person?

....

....

....

Find additional copies of this page on your CD.